Table of Contents

Book One:

THE LOST ART OF INTERCESSION

by James W. Goll

Book Two:

POWER THROUGH PRAYER

E.M. Bounds

BOOK ONE

THE LOST
Art OF INTERCESSION

Restoring the Power and Passion
of the Watch of the Lord

JAMES W. GOLL

Acknowledgment

Over the years, I have had the high privilege of being impacted by some of the greatest teachers and generals of prayer. Their deposits into my life have been rich and irreplaceable. But, it is to the "little butlers" that I owe the most thanks to. I thank the Lord for all those sacrificial servants who have helped to hold up my arms as we continue with endurance to run the race that is set before us.

I have also had the blessing of a family who has released and blessed me to be all that I can be in God, to be the unique vessel God has created me to be. I want to thank my family—especially my parents, Wayne and Amanda Goll—who both have gone on to be with the Lord in recent years. Thanks for marking my life with the spirit of prayer for our King.

Endorsements

"Authority and power reside in this book because it comes out of a life that has 'done,' and then taught. Finally, these precious, forged gems are out before us. Feast your eyes and let these truths change your life! Get ready to take a ride into new dimensions of intercession and worship in your personal and corporate prayer life."

Wesley Tullis
Director, Manna Relief
Dallas, Texas

"James Goll is one of the most passionate, intercessory-prophetic persons, regarding the things of God, whom I have met. His teachings have been very helpful to me and I know they will be very enriching to those who read this book."

Randy Clark
Global Awakening Team Leader
Harrisburg, PA

"If you want to be consumed on the altar of God, if you want your heart to be enlarged for God's full purposes in our generation, then you will profit from this book. The Psalmist says that God confides in those who fear Him. The Lord confides different things to different people so that we need each other to become whole. James W. Goll fears the Lord and the Lord has confided some things to him that I needed. You need them too."

Dr. Don Finto
Pastor, Caleb Company
Nashville, Tennessee

"James Goll has had a significant impact on my life personally and on that of Harvest Rock Church. He's a man who hears from God and has the character to obey accordingly. I highly commend what he has to say about the urgency and art of intercession in this crucial hour."

Che Ahn, D. Min.
Senior Pastor, Harvest Rock Church
Founder of Harvest International Ministries
Pasadena, California

"I have known James Goll for more than 25 years, and I appreciate his passion for Jesus and gifting in intercession and the prophetic. Jim was the Director of the School of the Spirit at our Grace Training Center in Kansas City for six years, and his classes were among the favorites of our students."

Mike Bickle
Director, International House of Prayer
Kansas City, Missouri
Author of *Passion for Jesus*

"Enough cannot be said for James W. Goll's latest addition to the arsenal of profound yet practical books on prayer. *The Lost Art of Intercession* is not some dry, academic treatise on prayer. No! It pulsates with prophetic life, complete with angelic visitations, visions, and miracles. It's just plain exciting stuff! Also, knowing both James and Michal Ann as I do, these stories are not merely the secondhand recitation of other people's experiences, but rather firsthand visitations like those in Bible days. I've heard many people speak and teach on prayer, but James Goll is one of the best yet. Don't let this book get by you."

Wesley and Stacey Campbell
Co-founders of Revival Now! Ministries
Kelowna, British Columbia, Canada

"'We are epistles written and read of all men.' What makes this book credible is not only its insight into the ministry of intercession, but also the author. James is no novice—he is a seasoned warrior. His writings are not the gleanings of a researcher; rather they are the lessons gained in the trenches of experience. James lives the life of an intercessor—read and follow his example."

David Ravenhill
Teacher
Lindale, Texas
Author of *For God's Sake, Grow Up!*

Foreword

In January of 1995 the Lord said to us, **"Watch with Me."** In response we invited about 20 people to spend from 10:00 P.M. Friday till 6:00 A.M. Saturday keeping the "Night Watch," which is going without sleep for spiritual reasons. We waited on God in worship and prayer and shared in communion through Jesus' body and blood in the Lord's Supper. Every Friday night since then we have done the same. We have celebrated the Watch with as many as 4,000 watchmen present. Watch groups are now springing up here and abroad. We find ourselves in the midst of a renewed visitation that is manifesting the glory of the Lord!

Prayer is the backbone of the Church. God is restoring our spiritual genetics as we keep the Watch. We are experiencing a new dimension of communion with the Lord. He is redefining our understanding of prayer.

The Lord is speaking a new word about an old word. The old word is **"Pray!"** The new word is **"Pray corporately!"** The Lord is opening our eyes to this simple truth: *Prayer is where everything begins and ends in the realm of the spirit.* It is where everything is accomplished. Prayer is the true genetic

15

code of the Church. We have experienced other mutant genes that have caused us to evolve away from God's true design for His Body. *But nothing God is going to do will happen without prayer.*

Watching is a historical part of every great ministry and every great revival. An excerpt from John Wesley's journal of 1739 reads:

> Mr. Hall, Kinchin, Ingham, Whitefield, Hutchins, and my brother Charles were present at our love-feast at Fetter Lane, with about sixty of our brethren. At about three in the morning, as we were continuing instant in prayer, the power of God came mightily upon us, inasmuch that many cried out for exceeding joy, and many fell to the ground. As soon as we recovered a little from that awe and amazement at the presence of His majesty, we broke out with one voice, "We praise Thee, O God; we acknowledge Thee to be the Lord!"[1]

Joel and the people of Israel, Wesley, the Moravians, and other groups have pioneered in all-night prayer. They tilled the ground and planted the seeds of God's heart for corporate prayer. God is now watering the seeds of revival and raising up watchmen to reap a new harvest through prayer.

One of the watchmen the Lord has been raising up is Jim Goll. It has been Bonnie's and my privilege to be intimately involved in the lives of Jim and Michal Ann Goll for several years. We love their passionate hunger for seeing a generation of prayer warriors arise.

In February of 1996 at a conference where we both ministered, I sent forth a call for "watchmen to take their stand on the wall." One of the first in line was, of course, my dear friend, Jim Goll. As he stood before me as a soldier waiting for his next orders, the Holy Spirit rose up inside me and I released a proclamation, "You are called as a General in the Watch of the Lord!" Little did I know at the time that Jim would be used to write this needed book on *The Lost Art of Intercession: Restoring the Power and Passion of the Watch of the Lord.* It is with great joy that I commend this book to you.

As the watchmen of the Lord, we are standing in the breaches and keeping the night vigil for deliverance and revival for our people, our nations, and our world. We hope that you will join us on the wall of prayer in keeping the **Watch of the Lord**.

Mahesh Chavda
Mahesh Chavda Ministries International
All Nations Church
Charlotte, North Carolina

ENDNOTE

1. *The Works of John Wesley* (Jackson), reprint ed. (Kansas City: Beacon Hill Press, 1979), 170, accessed on the Internet at: http://wesley.nnu.edu/wesleyan_theology/theojrnl/31-35/32-2-3.htm#Nine.

Introduction

Are you hungry for authentic revival in the land? Does your heart burn with a passion to see Jesus receive the rewards of His suffering? Do you want to do the works of Christ? If so, then I think God had you in mind when He prompted me to write *The Lost Art of Intercession*.

I need to tell you from the start that I am determined to infect you with a holy disease and a righteous obsession. I hope you become a total *prayeraholic*! I believe God wants to see a whole generation of humble, priestly people rise up with the passion and anointing to lay hold of God as He has laid hold of them. I desperately want to see this dream come to pass.

By the grace of God the original manuscript of *The Lost Art of Intercession* has touched the lives of thousands around the world and has been one of the tools to help ignite the greatest global prayer movement the Church has ever seen. The copy you hold in your hand is a new release with added material to even better equip you. Not only have I reedited the book to make it up to date, but we added a section taken from the writings of pastor, intercessor and writer E. M. Bounds.

Edward McKendree Bounds (1835-1913), Methodist minister and devotional writer, was born in Shelby County, Missouri. He studied law and was admitted to the bar at age 21. After practicing law for three years, he began preaching for the Methodist Episcopal Church, South. At the time of his pastorate at Brunswick, Missouri, was declared, and he was made a prisoner of war for refusing to take the oath of allegiance to the Federal Government. After his release he served as chaplain of the Fifth Missouri regiment (for the Confederate Army) until the close of the war, when he was captured and held prisoner at Nashville, Tennessee.

E. M. Bounds led the troops in intercession and eventually pastored in my home town of Franklin, Tennessee. In fact, he led the troops marching down Henpeck Lane in Franklin, right where our Encounters Ministry Center is today. I have studied this man's prayerful life and found the following parallels to my own.

We were both Missourians and came from a Methodist church heritage. We both pastored in Missouri and had a spirit of prayer upon our lives. We both moved to Franklin to help lead in prayer during a time of war. Interesting, eh? So, in a book on restoring the power and the passion of the watch of the Lord, it seemed appropriate to add vintage material from one of our great forerunners.

As you read these words, Jesus Christ continuously intercedes for you and the Church before His Father. *And He invites you to do the same.* According to Romans 8:34 and Hebrews 7:25, this ministry of intercession is continuous and unbroken.

Jesus, our magnificent obsession, is our most excellent advocate (defense attorney, representative, and go-between) with the Father. He took His stand between us and our sin, and He remains the Intercessor who stands between us and our arch enemy, satan. He personally identified with our total depravity and took upon Himself the sins of every human generation. Then Jesus, the unblemished and guiltless Lamb of God, carried our sin to the cross and forever removed it by dying the death of the guilty man of sin so we would be free. He has done it all!

Jesus Christ wants you and I to join Him there in the Father's Presence. Will you join Him in "this road less traveled"? He is searching throughout the earth for spiritual adventurers who will search and excavate for lost treasures of the Holy kind. Will you pay the price to help restore the glory of God to the earth? Do you want to join me? Then read on, brave soul. This book was written just for you.

James W. Goll, Author
Encounters Network
Author of *The Seer, The Lost Art of Practicing His Presence,
Dream Language* and many more

CHAPTER 1

Restoring the Moravian Fire

Like Ezekiel of old who sat in the valley filled with old bones, we were sitting in a great cemetery filled with gravestones that marked the resting place of hundreds of Moravian saints. These nearly forgotten prayer warriors had pioneered some of the richest and most daring missionary workin the history of the Church, but on this day all was silent.

Drawn there by a prophetic mission on that pleasant afternoon in February of 1993, 19 intercessors, including my wife, Michal Ann, and myself, paused for prayer before completing our walk through the cemetery. Our goal was to reach the wooden prayer tower overlooking the cemetery and the Moravian village of Herrnhut, which is located on the southeastern border of Germany, across from Poland and the Czech Republic. While sitting in the cemetery during that time of somber prayer, the Lord spoke to my heart, "Son of man, can these bones live?"

And I responded with the same answer given by Ezekiel thousands of years before me, "Sovereign Lord, You alone know."

Moments later, we quietly left the cemetery and climbed the hill to the prayer tower. After I unlocked the door, we climbed a spiral staircase to the circular mezzanine at the top of the Moravian watchtower. From that vantage point, we could see far beyond the borders of eastern Germany into the neighboring Czech Republic and Poland, but some invisible hand seemed to

---

We had called forth the winds of God's anointing, and that wind was blowing among us.

We sensed that it bore with it the same anointing that God once gave to the Moravian prayer warriors of the eighteenth century!

---

draw us all away from simply viewing. As we silently gathered together in a loose circle, we could sense a weightiness and deep anticipation growing in our hearts. Something was about to happen.

Suddenly, every person in the tower was overwhelmed with a compelling spirit of intercession unlike anything we had ever experienced. As we prayed, agonized, and groaned under the obvious influence of the Holy Spirit, a strong wind suddenly blew about the tower where we were standing, whipping away hats and scarves in its power. We all knew that this natural phenomenon was an outward manifestation of a mighty movement by the Spirit of God.

As one person, we were gripped in deep, groaning travail. We knew what was happening. We had traveled tens of thousands of miles as a team and experienced incredible provision and guidance all along our journey to fulfill the Holy Spirit's command. Our mission was to seek God for the anointing of the spirit of prayer that once rested upon Count Nikolaus Ludwig von Zinzendorf and the Moravian community of faith. Now, just as the prophet Ezekiel called forth the winds of God in Ezekiel 37, we had called forth the winds of God's anointing, and that wind was blowing among us. We sensed that it bore with it the same anointing that God once gave to the Moravian prayer warriors of the eighteenth century!

When the wind died down, we waited. Was our mission complete? Was it over as quickly as it began? Somehow we all knew that God wasn't finished with us yet. We confirmed it later, but at the time we sensed that as a woman in the midst of giving birth, we were in a lull between "contractions." Suddenly, we were hit spontaneously as one person with an even stronger spirit of travail, and a second wind began to roar across the valley and up the prayer tower mezzanine where we were positioned. I sensed that this second wind had brought a new wave of faith and anointing to fulfill a holy mandate to blow this spirit of prayer out into the nations.

Immediately, I felt an impression "light up" inside of me that God wanted to raise up the "house of prayer for all nations" in 120 cities, just as He breathed His Spirit into the 120 prayer warriors on the day of Pentecost (see Matt. 21:13; Acts 2). From those 120 cities of prayer, God intended to cover the earth with His glory.

Nearly everything in my life had been leading up to that divine appointment with God in Herrnhut. I knew that the rest of my days would be influenced by what transpired that day in a tower above the graves of Count von Zinzendorf and the Moravian brethren.

THREE STRANDS OF TRUTH

What did the believers at Herrnhut have that we don't have today?

Long before I ever set foot in the Czech Republic (formerly part of Czechoslovakia) for the first time, I had read books and articles describing the Christian community commonly called the "Moravians." Their story is intertwined with the lives and ministries of some of the most important church leaders in the Great Awakenings and revivals that transformed

Western society in the eighteenth century. I learned that God gave them "three strands" around which they wove their lives, and these strands helped the Moravians become world-changers:

1. **They had relational unity, spiritual community, and sacrificial living.**

2. **The power of their persistent prayer produced a divine passion and zeal for missionary outreach to the lost.** Many of them even sold themselves into slavery in places like Surinam in South America just so they could carry the light of the gospel into closed societies. The Moravians were the first missionaries to the slaves of St. Thomas in the Virgin Islands; they went to strange places called Lapland and Greenland and to many places in Africa.

3. **The third strand was described by a motto that they lived by: "No one works unless someone prays."** This took the form of a corporate commitment to sustained prayer and ministry to the Lord. This prayer went on unbroken for 24 hours a day, seven days a week, every day of each year for over 100 years!

The Moravians' over 100-year prayer vigil and global missionary exploits marked one of the purest moves of the Spirit in church history, and it radically changed the expression of Christianity in their age. Many leaders today feel that virtually every great missionary endeavor of the eighteenth and nineteenth centuries—regardless of denominational affiliation—was in a very real sense part of the fruit of the Moravians' sacrificial service and prophetic intercessory prayer. Their influence continues to be felt even in our day. The Lord is clearly planning to increase that influence once again.

Just as the 120 believers tarrying in the upper room in Jerusalem on Pentecost were "baptized in fire" by the Holy Spirit of promise, so those who answer God's call to tarry before His face will also be baptized with a holy fire. The group of believers who gathered at Herrnhut to pursue their dream of religious freedom were in much the same state as most Christians are today. They came from widely diverse religious backgrounds. During the first five years of their communal existence after the community's founding in 1722, they experienced bickering, dissension, and strife. They were no better or worse than you or I, but they made a deep commitment to Jesus Christ and to prayer, which transformed and changed them forever. They began to think God-sized thoughts and feel a burning, God-like compassion for the lost. They received supernatural faith to tackle challenges that would, in many cases, cost them their freedom or their very lives. Yet, they did it all in faithfulness and joy.

The Moravians changed the world because they allowed God to change them. God wants to change the world again and He is looking at you and me. Are you willing to seek the same fire that inspired the Moravian believers two centuries ago?

The joy and peaceful confidence that the Moravians exhibited in the face of adversity and death was legendary. "Count von Zinzendorf taught the Moravians to be God's troubadours: They first looked at the Cross and rejoiced because they found there a covering for all their sins. Zinzendorf once declared: 'We are the Saviour's happy people'…The Moravians have been called the 'Easter People,' and perhaps no other body of Christians has so compellingly expressed their adoration of the risen Lamb."[1]

WESLEY'S ENCOUNTER

John Wesley first encountered Moravians during a stormy ocean voyage. Their influence was destined to forever transform his life and ultimately helped to launch the Great Awakening that swept through England and America! Author and prophetic teacher, Rick Joyner, recently published a booklet titled *Three Witnesses*, which describes the miraculous work of the Moravians along with their effect on John Wesley in particular:

> During January 1736, Wesley was on a ship bound for America that also carried a number of Moravian missionaries. He was challenged by their great seriousness and their humility in performing for other passengers the most servile tasks, which none of the English passengers would do. When they were offered pay for this, they refused, replying that "it was good for their proud hearts," and "their loving Savior had done more for them." Some of the passengers

abused them terribly, even striking them or knocking them down, but they would never strike back or even take offense.

Many perceived these German missionaries as cowards until a great storm broke over the ship. As the main sail split and the sea began to pour into the ship, the English panicked, their terrified screams rising even above the tumult of the storm. Yet the Moravians sat quietly, singing their hymns. Afterwards, when one of the Moravians was asked if he was afraid during the storm, he answered, "I thank God, no." Then he was asked if their women and children were afraid, and he replied, "No; our women and children are not afraid to die." Wesley recorded this in his diary and added:

"From them [the Moravians] I went to their crying, trembling neighbors, and pointed out to them the difference in the hour of trial, between him that feareth God, and him that feareth not. At twelve the wind fell. This was the most glorious day which I have hitherto seen."[2]

Wesley knew that he didn't possess what he saw in those simple people of faith, those people called Moravians. He was an ordained minister, yet he hadn't even received Christ as his Savior. He was fascinated by the Moravians' confidence in the face of impending death. He knew that he didn't have what they had, and he decided that he wanted it—whatever it was.

The fire of the Moravian believers seemed to ignite hunger for God wherever they went. That hunger could only be satisfied by an encounter with the living God they served. Would to God that every believer, missionary, and minister today would walk, work, and worship with the same fire that the Moravians carried with them to countless cultures and cities!

God is out to ignite that fire again! Only this time He wants to see His fire roar across entire continents and cultures through the means of His whole Body, the Church. As you read these words, the Spirit of God is igniting hearts around the world, drawing believers to their knees and sinners to the cross. He is out to cover the earth with the Father's glory, but He has been

*John Wesley was an ordained minister,
yet he hadn't even received Christ as his Savior.*

*He was fascinated by the Moravians' confidence
in the face of impending death.*

*He knew that he didn't have what they had,
and he decided that he wanted it—whatever it was.*

commissioned to do it through the transformed lives of fallen human beings who have been redeemed by the blood of Jesus Christ, the Lamb of God.

There is an incident involving Aaron, the priest, and the fire of God that pictures the burden of my heart for this book and the work of God in this generation. It is found in Numbers 16:

> *And the Lord spoke to Moses, saying, "Get away from among this congregation, that I may consume them instantly." Then they fell on their faces. Moses said to Aaron,* **"Take your censer and put in it fire from the altar, and lay incense on it; then bring it quickly to the congregation and make atonement** *for them, for wrath has gone forth from the Lord, the plague has begun!" Then Aaron took it as Moses had spoken, and* **ran into the midst of the assembly,** *for behold, the plague had begun among the people. So he put on the incense and made atonement for the people. And* **he took his stand between the dead and the living,** *so that the plague was checked. But those who died by the plague were 14,700, besides those who died on account of Korah* (Numbers 16:44-49).

Aaron provides a vivid picture of the intercessor. When the congregation of Israel sinned by rebelling against their leaders, God sent a judgment upon them in the form of a plague that killed nearly 15,000 people. Far more would have died, but Moses told Aaron, the high priest, to quickly put fire from God's altar into his censer, or container, along with incense. Then Aaron literally ran out into the midst of the congregation with the fire of God. The Scripture says that Aaron "took his stand between the dead and the living." The fragrant smoke ascending from the burning censer, as Aaron swung it to and fro, formed a line of demarcation between two groups—the dead and the living.

WHAT ARE THE APPLICATIONS FOR TODAY?

What does that mean for us? I attended a Russian Orthodox service in an effort to better understand the principles in this Old Testament passage. The word *cantor* refers to a priest who prays and sings chants. If you have ever heard a Gregorian chant sung with power and anointing, then you know how beautiful and absolutely incredible the song of a cantor can be. The cantor has a censer or a cantor, a container, a can that is filled with incense. Throughout the cantor's ministry, it continually releases a sweet fragrance and smoke that will fill the sanctuary. Many times this cantor-priest will be dressed in royal priestly regalia as he walks among the people with his instruments of sacrifice (the censer and incense). I remember the Russian Orthodox cantor singing from the Psalms in high praise, "The Lord is good. And His mercy endures forever."

Then I heard the people say with one voice, "Amen. The Lord is good, and His mercy endures forever. Amen."

What I saw in the Orthodox service was what I believe to be a very accurate picture of what Aaron did. However, on the day of the crisis when Aaron stepped close to the shekinah presence of God in the Holy of Holies to take of the fire on the altar, I believe he became consumed with the zeal of the Lord of Hosts and he became a radical!

That is what God wants to do with you and me, and with everyone who calls upon the name of the Lord. He wants to break off the power of intimidation in our lives and cast down the spirit of fear that rejects and avoids the unknown. I once heard my friend, Paul Cain, one of the leading prophetic statesmen of our day, say, "One of the problems we have is that we are so afraid of wildfire that we have no fire." God wants His Kingdom of kings and priests to once again take the fire from His presence and rush it with godly zeal to the people in need. All you have to do is find an "altar" where the fire of God is burning along with an abundant supply of sweet

---

God wants His Kingdom of kings and priests to once again take the fire from His presence and rush it with godly zeal to the people in need.

All you have to do is find an "altar" where the fire of God is burning along with an abundant supply of sweet incense.

---

incense. He wants to transform our generation through His shekinah glory, just as He transformed Aaron.

God wants to use more than a Moses or an Aaron today. One of the unique things about the Church of the New Covenant is that God has authorized and commanded *every believer* to do the work of the ministry! "Point people," or church leaders, can't do it all; in fact, their primary job or reason for being, according to the apostle Paul, is *"for the equipping of the saints for the work of service, to the building up of the body of Christ"* (Eph. 4:12). God wants an entire army of workers out doing the vital work of the ministry and building up His Body, the Church.

The plague in Numbers chapter 16 was stopped because Aaron stood in the gap. That is the classic definition of an intercessor: "one who stands in the gap for another." Aaron stood in the gap for his generation, and the plague was stopped. There is a devilish plague running rampant today through our churches, cities, and nations. Now the Lord is calling for a priestly people to rise up and personally carry the holy fire of His presence to their generation for their salvation and His glory.

WHO WILL STAND IN THE GAP?

Let me bring this a little closer to home: God wants to put His Spirit upon you in such a measure that you will answer His summons with a resounding: "Yes, I will stand in the gap for my generation right here and now. I will put aside every pathetic intimidation and every entanglement of namby-pamby religion. I am going to make a difference by willingly taking up the cross of an intercessor. I will lay aside my life for the sake of others before God."

God is restoring the ancient fire that once inspired the Moravians to launch what, in their day, was the greatest missionary campaign since the Book of Acts. He is restoring His fire to you and me in this generation because He wants us to reap His harvest. The first step begins with the restoration of the fire on God's altar.

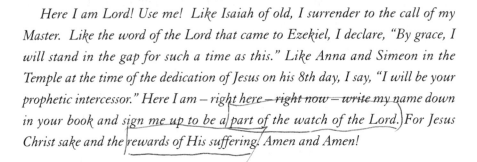

Here I am Lord! Use me! Like Isaiah of old, I surrender to the call of my Master. Like the word of the Lord that came to Ezekiel, I declare, "By grace, I will stand in the gap for such a time as this." Like Anna and Simeon in the Temple at the time of the dedication of Jesus on his 8th day, I say, "I will be your prophetic intercessor." Here I am – right here – right now – write my name down in your book and sign me up to be a part of the watch of the Lord. For Jesus Christ sake and the rewards of His suffering. Amen and Amen!

ENDNOTES

1. Anthony J. Lewis, *Zinzendorf the Ecumenical Pioneer* (London: S.C.M. Press, 1962), 73-74.

2. Rick Joyner, *Three Witnesses* (Charlotte, NC: Morningstar Publications, 1997), 56.

CHAPTER 2

Restoring the Fire on the Altar

Fire shall be kept burning continually on the altar; it is not to go out (Leviticus 6:13).

Several years ago the Lord called me aside to spend nearly a month with Him in "solitary confinement." His purpose was clear: He wanted to place me in an intensive "Mary position" so I could hear clearly what He wanted to say to me.[1] I didn't realize it then, but the words I would hear at the end of those weeks of isolated prayer would lay part of the foundation for my ministry during the remainder of this decade, and for this book as well. I came to learn later that He was also saying the same thing to other members of His Body around the world.

I suspended my travel itinerary and positioned myself far from the nearest telephone. (The voice I needed to hear did not need a telephone or e-mail to reach me.) During that period, I spent precious hours waiting on the Lord, and He blessed me again and again as I sat at His feet and listened for His every word. At the end of my prayer consecration, the Holy Spirit gave me an order from the Father's throne: "It's time for *fire on the altar.*"

I had been awakened in the night a few months earlier, and for two hours my mind had been filled with eight phrases that kept circulating in my thoughts as I sought God's face: "Blazing altars…the fire and the altar…altars ablaze…flaming altars…the altar and the flame…altars aflame…altars on fire." The one phrase that struck me the most was, "Fire on the altar." I didn't realize it at the time, but this was an exact quote of a portion of Leviticus 6:9, which says, *"Command Aaron and his sons, saying, 'This is the law for the burnt offering: the burnt offering itself shall remain on the hearth on the altar all night until the morning, and the **fire on the altar** is to be kept burning on it.'"*

---

*Count von Zinzendorf knew the fire of
the altar signified the prayer of the saints,
and he viewed this Word as a literal command
to restore unceasing prayer before the Lord.*

*Church history, and, therefore, world
history, would never be the same again.*

This is followed four verses later by the summary command, *"Fire shall be kept burning continually on the altar; it is not to go out"* (Lev. 6:13). According to Professor Leslie K. Tarr, this is the verse that Count von Zinzendorf received from the Holy Spirit in 1727, which inspired the Moravian's incredible 100-year prayer vigil launched that year.[2] The Count realized that this reference referred to the altar of sacrifice, but he also understood that this Old Testament priestly function involving fire and sacrifices carried a much greater and abiding significance on this side of the Cross. He knew that the fire of the altar signified the *prayer of the saints,* and he viewed this word as a literal command to restore unceasing prayer before the Lord. Church history, and, therefore, world history, would never be the same again.

One of the weaknesses I perceive in many North American churches today is a profound ignorance—and even a disdain, at times—of the Old

Testament Scriptures. It is not surprising that few American believers understand the Book of Hebrews or the many references of Jesus Christ that come from the Old Testament. Anyone who longs to walk closer to God must embrace *all* of His Word, including the books of the Old Testament. Count von Zinzendorf's revelation from the Book of Leviticus is an important example of how God can use shadows and types from Old Testament relationships and dealings to reveal and enlighten us on His work today.

According to the instructions that Aaron, the high priest, received through Moses in Leviticus chapter 16, before the high priest could pass through the inner veil into the Most Holy Place (or *Holy of Holies*), he was supposed to minister at two stations in the outer court and three within the Holy Place. First, he would offer up the sacrifice of blood at the brazen altar. This was followed by the ceremonial washing of water at the laver. After entering the Holy Place through the outer veil, the priest would approach the lamp stand (which held seven golden candlesticks), the table of shewbread, and the golden altar of incense, which rested immediately in front of the inner veil. Beyond the veil in the Most Holy Place was the ark of the covenant, with the mercy seat flanked by its covering cherubs. This was the place of communion—the place where God's presence was manifested and His glory was made known.

GOD'S PROPHETIC CALENDAR

Where do we stand corporately in God's prophetic timetable? The stations of service in the tabernacle of Moses perfectly picture the progressive work of God to perfect His Bride in the earth. The Protestant Reformation restored the spiritual truths depicted by the brazen altar and its blood sacrifice. This simple yet profound understanding of justification by faith in the blood of Christ is the beginning place in our journey into the presence of God.

In the 1800s, John Wesley and the Holiness Movement helped to reclaim the spiritual truths of the laver: the place of cleansing and sanctification. At the turn of the century, the Pentecostal Revival returned the emphasis of the power and the gifts of the Spirit as represented in the lamp stand (or the seven golden candlesticks). Sixty years later this was followed by the Charismatic

Renewal, which highlighted the fellowship of breaking bread as exhibited in the table of shewbread.

Perhaps today, in God's progressive plan of unfolding truth, we find ourselves ministering at the altar of incense. As the New Testament priesthood of believers, we are prophetically swinging the censer of praise and prayers unto the Lord Most High. Today, we stand collectively before the altar of incense and the time for lighting our incense has come!

A LIFE-CHANGING EVENT

In January 1993, I traveled to the Czech Republic with a group of intercessors to join the believers there in "christening" their new nation to the Lord. While standing on the platform before Dan Drapal's Christian Fellowship of Prague, a series of words seemed to fall into my mind. "Have you considered the multidirectional dimension of prayer?" This sentence captured my attention but I did not have time to ponder it, as it was time for me to deliver my next statement. Then the words, "Remember, what goes up must come down!" burst into my conscience. What was the Lord trying to tell me? Does prayer have more than one direction? My thoughts quickly were then taken to Revelation 8:3-5:

> And another angel came and stood at the altar, holding a golden censer; and much incense was given to him, so that he might add it to the prayers of all the saints on the golden altar which was before the throne. And the smoke of the incense, with the prayers of the saints, went up before God out of the angel's hand. Then the angel took the censer and filled it with the fire of the altar, and threw it to the earth; and there followed peals of thunder and sounds and flashes of lightning and an earthquake (Revelation 8:3-5).

I could begin to see it. *What goes up does come down!* Our prayers arise from our humble earthly habitation unto their heavenly destination. The angels, acting as altar attendants, take their censers and fill them with much incense (which is the prayers of the saints). The angels become the heavenly cantors, swinging our prayers and praises before our Lord. Then they take the censers and fill them with the *fire on the altar* and throw it back down on the earth. Signs and wonders follow as what went up is cast back down on the earth.

One of these "wonders" that is specifically listed in Revelation 8 is lightning. Amazing, isn't it? Nearly a year later, God gave me another piece to the puzzle in a powerful dream I received in Toronto, Ontario. It concerned the "downward fire" of the godly equation, "What goes up must come down." I was conducting my second "Fire on the Altar Conference" at a Vineyard Fellowship in Cambridge, a suburb of Toronto, in December of 1993. My last night, in the basement guest room of the pastor's house, I had a dream in which I saw hundreds of consecutive lightning bolts splintering and showering down on the earth from the heavens. There weren't any people or spoken words in the dream, just this brilliant shower of lightning bolts continuously striking the earth.

I don't know what time it was, but some time that night I awoke from the dream and realized that the room was filled with what I call "the destiny of God." Then, with my eyes wide open, I saw large letters measuring two or three feet high hanging in the room, and they said, "Job 36:32." I just waited quietly in the room, and after a while I turned on the light and reached for my Bible. I was thrilled and puzzled by what I read in verse 32 and the following verses.

> *He covers His hands with the lightning, and commands it to strike the mark. Its noise declares His presence; the cattle also, concerning what is coming up. At this also my heart trembles, and leaps from its place. Listen closely to the thunder of His voice, and the rumbling that goes out from His mouth. Under the whole heaven He lets it loose, and His lightning to the ends of the earth* (Job 36:32–37:3).

God covers His hands with *lightning* and He sends it forth and it strikes the mark. Although these are the words of Elihu, they sure seem to agree with the picture of God's fire in Revelation 8:3-5. Later I came to learn that the Hebrew word translated as "strikes the mark" is *paga*. This same word is translated as "intercession" in Isaiah 59:16, where God laments in the

Messianic passage, *"And He saw that there was no man, and was astonished that there was no one to **intercede** [paga]; then His own arm brought salvation to Him; and His righteousness upheld Him."*

Intercession releases God's brilliant light or lightning to "strike the mark" in the earth, directing God's power and glory into desired situations with supernatural results! A friend sent me a lengthy study of lightning in the Bible and suggested that lightning is the anointed Word of God going forth from the mouth of the saints. He believed the Scriptures imply that as we speak the Word of God, it goes forth from our mouth like lightning to intercede and strike the mark, routing our enemies and bringing the judgment of God to situations, laying bare the hearts of men, and fully accomplishing whatever God commanded it to accomplish. I have to agree that this is totally in line with the Bible as I understand it.

THE POWER OF GOD'S WORD

When God's Word goes forth, channels of living water appear in the midst of barren deserts. God's Word lights up everything, and nothing can hide from its illuminating power. Demonic powers tremble and melt at its presence. When God's Word is sent forth in faith and obedience, it will cause people around us to see God's glory.

Another picture of this dynamic function of *paga* is that intercession "paints the targets" so God can zero in on areas of need with His glory! He sets His "gun sights" on these targets and "strikes the mark" with His lightning or "displays of His brilliant presence."[3] We have the privilege of painting targets on cities, nations, churches, and individuals granting access points to the One whose hands are covered with light. By this, we call light to overcome darkness.

This dream of the continuous shower of lightning bolts from Heaven came in December of 1993, seven weeks before the outbreak of the Spirit began after the Lord sent Randy Clark to what was then the Toronto Airport Vineyard Christian Fellowship. Since then, the rain of God's presence on that region has been continuous. A pastor's wife from the State of Washington was in a service in Toronto and "under the influence" of the Holy Spirit when the voice of the Lord whispered to her and said: "Do you remember all of the prayers that you have prayed for revival? This is the beginning of that." Since then, even the secular media has discovered the fires of God roaring out from places like Toronto, Canada, Pensacola, Florida, London, England and Pemba, Mozambique, Africa.

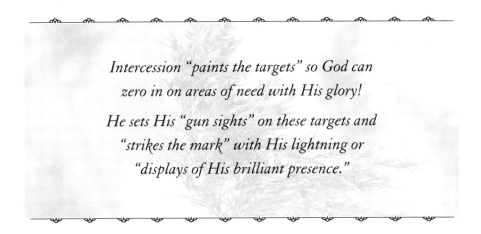

Intercession "paints the targets" so God can zero in on areas of need with His glory!

He sets His "gun sights" on these targets and "strikes the mark" with His lightning or "displays of His brilliant presence."

Not only is it amazing and astounding that our prayers affect the destiny of individuals and nations, but God would also say to us: "Rejoice that you are given the magnificent privilege of ministering to Me at this most precious heavenly altar! Rejoice that the altar of incense is that which is nearest to My heart." Oh, what a blessed gift and privilege is this holy thing called prayer!

More than anything else, prayer is man's invitation sent heavenward for God's response to be cast earthward—the human in exchange for the heavenly!

Second Chronicles 7:1-3 gloriously depicts this principle:

> *Now when Solomon had finished praying, fire came down from heaven and consumed the burnt offering and the sacrifices, and the glory of the Lord filled the house. The priests could not enter into the house of the Lord because the glory of the Lord filled the Lord's house. And all the sons of Israel, seeing the fire come down and the glory of the Lord upon the house, bowed down on the pavement with their faces to*

the ground, and they worshiped and gave praise to the Lord, saying, "Truly He is good, truly His lovingkindness is everlasting" (2 Chronicles 7:1-3).

This is what we yearn for! We have seen it happen here and there—in Smithton, Missouri; Sunderland, England; Bogata, Columbia; and Redding, California and then in many other cities across the globe. But we must have more, Lord! We want to see God's glory fill the earth. *It will happen through exchange.* Prayer ascends. Incense arises. Man's smoke signal to His Highest Chief arises declaring, "Send forth the fire!" Heavenly fire from the altar then comes crashing down and the glory of the Lord fills His house once again. What goes up must come down.

Let's present ourselves on God's altar as our spiritual service of worship. (See Romans 12.) Let's offer up the continual sacrifices of praise and the incense of prayer. And let us continue to do so until the angels take their censer, fill it to the brim, and cast Heaven's *fire on the altar* back down into our earthly dwelling places again.

Even so, let the fire on the altar come tumbling forth. Let God's priests prostrate themselves before Him. May His glory invade and pervade His house until all God's people cry, "Amen and Amen!"

FOLLOWING THE BLUEPRINT

The Old Testament "blueprint" of the tabernacle of Moses reveals an ancient and divine pattern marking the methodical restoration of truth and practice in Church history. The tabernacle was divided into three areas, and each area was equipped with specific pieces of furniture for specific purposes. The path to God's presence required the high priest of the Old Testament to move progressively from the outer court into the inner court (the Holy Place), and ultimately through the veil into the Holy of Holies, or the Most Holy Place. These steps of progressive revelation have a striking parallel to God's plan of restoration for His Son's Bride, the Church:

I. **The Outer Court—Where Sinful Man Comes to God in Need of Salvation**

A. The Protestant Reformation (Repentance and Forgiveness: First Station of the Lamb)

1. Restoration of the altar of sacrifice

2. Restoration of the sacrifice of the blood

3. Restoration of justification by faith

B. The Holiness Movement (Cleansing and Sanctification: Second Station of the Lamb)

1. Restoration of the brazen laver

2. Restoration of the washing of the hands

3. Restoration of cleansing and sanctification

II. **The Inner Court—The Holy Place (for Priests Only)**

A. The Pentecostal Outpouring (Illumination and Anointing: Third Station of the Lamb)

1. Restoration of the golden lamp stand

2. Restoration of the lighting and burning of the seven golden candlesticks

3. Restoration of the power and gifts of the Spirit

B. The Charismatic Outpouring (the Full Portion of God's Bread: Fourth Station of the Lamb)

1. Restoration of the table of shewbread

2. Restoration of the 12 loaves of bread, representing the 12 tribes of Israel

3. Restoration of fellowship across the Body of Christ

C. The Prayer Movement (Worship and Prayer: Fifth Station of the Lamb)

1. Restoration of the altar of incense

2. Restoration of the fire continually burning on the altar

3. Restoration of worship and prayer

The time of the incense has come! That the altar of incense has its place nearest to the curtain before the Holy of Holies signifies the spiritual specificity of prayer as coming nearest to the heart of God.

Perhaps the "sixth station" of the Lamb will be the unveiling of an entire Church of kings and priests ministering boldly to God Himself within the Most Holy Place—in full view of the unsaved world and the principalities and powers of the air. This would be a literal fulfillment of David's ancient psalm in which he said, *"The Lord is my Shepherd, I shall not want...He setteth a table before me in the presence of mine enemies"* (see Ps. 23).

I find it interesting that whether you ask people in worship services at Pasadena's Harvest Rock Church, London's Holy Trinity Brompton Anglican Church, or at Grace Center in Franklin, Tennessee, or at any of the other places where God's Spirit is being poured out, they will all speak in the same terms. They say they sensed God's glory and presence overwhelm them. This is one of the ways we experience the "manifest presence of God," which is exactly how the Old Testament describes the Presence that descended on the mercy seat between the golden cherubim of the ark of the covenant in Aaron's day! My friends, the God of Abraham, Isaac, and Jacob is alive and well today. He has arisen to visit His people by sitting in the throne of worship and prayer we have made for Him through our prayer, praise, worship, and intercession!

Sometimes God breaks out of our "theoretical models of prayer." You see, He is not a static God. He is not a "tame" God who is content to stay inside of our neat little theological boxes and paradigms. According to the Scriptures, when we dare to draw near to Him, He will draw near to us (see James 4:8)! That means that when you move yourself close to the consuming fire of God, then He will move the fire of His presence closer to you. That means that you and I are going to feel the heat of God and get fired up too!

IS YOUR HEART ON FIRE?

Consider the qualities of fire. In the natural realm, fire purifies, fuels, illuminates, and warms. In the spirit realm, fire is seen as the power of God to judge, sanctify, empower, inspire, enlighten, reveal, and warm the heart. It is time to draw near to the altar of God and stoke the fires of God in our hearts. There is another type of divine response to our uplifted fire and incense in addition to His dispatch of holy lightning to the earth:

> *Fire came down from Heaven and consumed the burnt offering and the sacrifices, and the glory of the Lord filled the house. And the priests could not enter into the house of the Lord, because the glory of the Lord filled the Lord's house* (2 Chronicles 7:1-2).

The restoration of the fire on the altar is not an end in itself. It is but the first step in a progression toward our loving God. In the next step, God wants to turn our eyes and hearts outward, from ourselves to others, with compassion like that of our great High Priest and Chief Intercessor.

I want to burn with the fire of God! Do not leave me the way I am. Consume me with the fire of your love for your holy name's sake. I want my heart to burn with the things that burn in your heart. I want to be numbered amongst your new Mary's of Bethany. Let the Spirit of prayer fall upon me this hour! I prayer this in the glorious name of Jesus!

ENDNOTES

1. The "Mary Position" is the posture of single-minded worship and yearning, while you are seated at the feet of Jesus with Him as your sole and total point of focus. This is in contrast to the approach of a "Martha." Martha busied herself with the details of work, and she is characterized by much distraction, worry, and care. Her busyness kept her apart from the words and face of Jesus (see Luke 10:38-42).

2. Leslie K. Tarr, "A Prayer Meeting That Lasted 100 Years," *Decision* (Billy Graham Evangelistic Association, May 1977). Used by permission.

3. This term, "brilliant presence," is part of another related vision concerning God's "highest weapon of spiritual warfare," which I cover in detail in Chapter 6 of this book, titled "Restoring the Path From Prayer to His Presence."

CHAPTER 3

Restoring the Priestly Role of Intercession

You also, as living stones, are being built up as a spiritual house for a
holy priesthood, to offer up spiritual sacrifices acceptable to God
through Jesus Christ (1 Peter 2:5).

Several years ago I was ministering in Phoenix, Arizona, when I saw a
vision take form in front of me. I saw a caterpillar that appeared to be weav-
ing something, and I realized it was forming a cocoon around itself. When
the time came for this caterpillar to finally emerge from its chrysalis, it had
to struggle just to escape its womb of transformation. Nevertheless, as I
watched, the creature struggled until it finally emerged as a fully formed
butterfly arrayed in brilliant and iridescent colors. When I asked the Lord
about what this was, He said, "It is the Church in metamorphosis."

Nearly everyone would agree at this point in time that the Church is in
a place of change. But if we are ever to reach the fullness of all that God has
prophesied we will be, then we must allow the Holy Spirit to tutor us and
lead us to the secret dwelling of the Most High God. It is there in His presence, hidden away from the world's influence, that we are changed into

another dimension and expression of His glory. We *all* have a divine appointment to be "shut in with God in a secret place." We are a priestly race in transition. We are called to press into God through Christ and overcome our fleshly encumbrances and worldly distractions so we can co-labor with Him to accomplish His plans and purposes. The Christian life is a life of change, of metamorphosis from the old to the new, of transformation "from glory to glory" as we look upon the face of God in the Most Holy Place. Then we will emerge from our holy seclusion arrayed with His iridescent glory, fully remade as many-faceted expressions of His love, His nature, and His glory. We know where and what we are now. But God has a plan—a blueprint—He is working from. Here is what God's Word says we should become:

> *You have made them to be a kingdom and priests to our God; and they will reign upon the earth* (Revelation 5:10).

> *For if by the transgression of the one, death reigned through the one, much more those who receive the abundance of grace and of the gift of righteousness will reign in life through the One, Jesus Christ* (Romans 5:17).

> *Therefore I urge you, brethren, by the mercies of God, to present your bodies a living and holy sacrifice, acceptable to God, which is your spiritual service of worship. And do not be conformed to this world, but be transformed by the renewing of your mind, so that you may prove what the will of God is, that which is good and acceptable and perfect* (Romans 12:1-2).

If there is one thing that I could plant in your heart, it would be this: Prayer is not an activity, and it is not an application. It is life found in a person. Once you see Jesus, once the blinders fall away from your eyes in the glory of His presence, your attitudes about prayer will totally change! This thing of prayer, this thing of intercession, of standing in the gap, of making an appeal to a superior—it is not a hard task! It is a joy. It's called life in the Kingdom.

The parallels between the duties of the Old Testament priests who served in the tabernacle of Moses and the priestly mission of believers today are too important to ignore or dismiss. Although the type of sacrifices we offer today and our reasons for offering them are dramatically different, it is still profitable to study the Old Testament priesthood. We can add to our knowledge and understanding of prayer by examining the priestly functions of the sons of Aaron, for those functions were instituted by God Himself, as a type and shadow of the greater priesthood of Jesus Christ and those who follow Him.

Throughout any study of Old Testament patterns, we should remember that every believer is called to be a priest unto the Lord today. Those duties are no longer confined to just a select few, and we need to understand that *there is no greater duty a believer can perform than prayer!* This is a chief function of the believer-priest today.

REMOVING THE BLOCKADES

In September of 1991, I was ministering in New York City with my wife, Michal Ann, when the presence of the Holy Spirit came to rest on me early one morning. I began to hear His voice clearly speaking the following words to me: "I will release new understandings of identification in intercession whereby the legal basis of the rights of the demonic powers of the air to remain will be removed. Then, in that hour My people will speak My Word and I will fell the enemy."

What is this "identification in intercession" anyway? I believe that it is a lost art, and it is perhaps one of the highest, yet most overlooked, aspects of true intercession. It is the ability and function of personally identifying with the needs of others to such an extent that in heart you become one with them by the Holy Spirit. It is expressed as we identify with Jesus and follow in His footsteps, because His footsteps will lead us beyond the four walls of our churches into the streets of a fractured world of prostitutes, crooks, losers, and broken and wounded people—in other words, to real people with real problems. He leads us into a genuine priesthood where we, like our Master and High Priest, can be touched by the infirmities, temptations, and struggles of others (see Heb. 4:15). The only way we can genuinely and effectively *intercede* is out of a heart of compassion, contrition, and desperation, from a heart that pounds with the sufferings of others as though they are our own. (To learn more on this subject of Identification in Intercession, please read book *Intercession – The Power and the Passion to Shape History*.)

Through the inward work of the Spirit of revelation, we can identify with God's righteous judgments, which are due, and yet experience His searing passion to express His grace and mercy. Our eyes will be opened to the horrifying condition of the people and the specific sins that block their way to the cross. Then, *by choosing to be one with them*, by laying aside our position for the sake of others, our hearts will be burdened by the Spirit of God to utter cries of confession and unspeakable intercession on their behalf. As we, from our hearts, confess sin, disgrace, failure, and humiliation on their behalf to the Lord, we

What is this "identification in intercession" anyway?
I believe that it is a lost art, and perhaps one of the highest,
yet most overlooked, aspects of true intercession.
It is the ability and function of personally identifying
with the needs of others to such an extent that
in heart you become one of them by the Holy Spirit.

clear away every obstacle of the enemy so that those for whom we labor can, themselves, come to the cross in repentance and restoration.

This form of intercession is a lost art in our modern-day materialistic and success-oriented society. This effective form of prayer includes confessing generational sins as you stand in the gap as an ambassador of your ethnic group, city, church or even your nation. We need more people with a heart like the apostle Paul, who wrote in the anguish of a true intercessor:

I am telling the truth in Christ, I am not lying, my conscience testifies with me in the Holy Spirit, that I have great sorrow and unceasing grief in my heart. **For I could wish that I myself were accursed, separated from Christ** *for the sake of my brethren, my kinsmen according to the flesh* (Romans 9:1-3).

Let's seek Him for these deeper workings in our lives so that *in our day* the Lord, the Judge of all, will find us standing in the gap for the Church, for our nation, and for the needy and the lost. Perhaps identification in intercession is the wedding of the spirit of revelation, described in Ephesians 1:7-8, with the spirit of conviction described by Jesus, who would convict the world of *"sin, and righteousness, and judgment"* (see John 16:8).

The Holy Spirit illuminated certain Scriptures with new understanding in the light of the word I received in New York City, particularly this passage in the Book of Isaiah:

And it shall be said, "Build up, build up, prepare the way. Remove every obstacle out of the way of My people." For thus says the high and exalted One who lives forever, whose name is Holy, "I dwell on a high and holy place, and also with the contrite and lowly of spirit in order to revive the spirit of the lowly and to revive the heart of the contrite" (Isaiah 57:14-15).

The Spirit wants to take Scripture passages like this and wed them with revelation and conviction. Then He will bring to us prophetic revelation and understanding and show how to use God's Word as a "holy bulldozer" to push out of the way the obstacle of sin and annul the curse over the land.

Paul wrote, *"But whom you forgive anything, I forgive also; for indeed what I have forgiven, if I have forgiven anything, I did it for your sakes in the presence of Christ, so that* **no advantage would be taken of us by satan; for we are not ignorant of his schemes"** (2 Cor. 2:10-11). God wants us to pray and intercede with great power and effectiveness, not foolishly striking blindly at the air like a poorly trained boxer (see 1 Cor. 9:26). The Holy Spirit wants to teach us how to "remove the legal basis of the demonic powers of the air to remain," so every devilish obstacle will be removed.

The passion of intercession springs from the heart of Jesus Christ Himself, who said, *"Behold, I say to you, lift up your eyes, and look on the fields, that they are white for harvest"* (John 4:35b). I think Jesus is saying something here that we don't normally comprehend. If we truly lift up our eyes to see with God's eyes, our vision is going to be filled with the horrifying condition of hurting people who are separated from Christ! In one sense, we don't need to ask God for a special "burden" to go into the fields. We need only open our eyes to see people as God sees them. Then our hearts will be moved with a burning compassion that stems directly from the Father heart of God.

PICTURES OF PRIESTHOOD

The roots of our high priestly ministry extend thousands of years behind us, preceding and foreshadowing the intent of God's invasion of human history through His Son, Jesus Christ. The first priest recorded in Scripture may well have been Adam, who ministered on behalf of God and God's creation in the garden of Eden. Then perhaps we see it in the accepted sacrifice of Abel. But the first individual actually called kohen, or priest, was Melchizedek, king of Salem:

> ... [who] *brought out bread and wine; now he was a priest of God Most High. He blessed him and said, "Blessed be Abram of God Most High, Possessor of heaven and earth; and blessed be God Most High, who has delivered your enemies into your hand." He gave him a tenth of all* (Genesis 14:18-20).

Even the first priest was careful to minister in two dimensions: to God on behalf of men, and to men on behalf of God. God later established the Aaronic priesthood as part of the instructions He gave to Moses on Mount Sinai, where He also gave him the law inscribed on stone tablets. He told Moses to build a tent according to very specific guidelines as His portable habitation among His people while they journeyed to the promised land. This tent was called the "tent of God's presence" and the tabernacle of Moses. It contained three main concentric areas into which only the priests of the tribe of Levi could enter, and then only after they had made themselves ceremonially clean.

The first area, just inside the curtains of the tent, was the courtyard or "outer place." The largest of the three spaces, it contained the brazen altar and brazen laver where the blood of innocent animal sacrifices without flaws was shed, and where their bodies were offered to God by fire. (The shedding of blood and the sacrifice of the innocent for the guilty in those sacrifices foreshadowed the shedding of Christ's innocent blood and His willing sacrifice on the Cross to take away the sin of the world.)

It was at the brazen laver that the bloodied priests washed themselves before moving deeper into the tent. Next was the main tent, a covered area that housed the Holy Place and the enclosed third area called the Most Holy Place (or Holy of Holies), where God's shekinah glory or presence resided. These spaces represented levels of holiness on earth. The deeper that one moved into the tabernacle, the stricter the requirements for holiness were.

Priests ministering under the old covenant followed a progressive series of rituals to prepare themselves to minister before the presence of the Holy God in the tabernacle. First, sacrifices of blood were offered for the atonement of sin in the outer court. The priest was required to first come to the place of sacrifice before he could enter the tabernacle and minister to the Lord. Only after Aaron, the high priest, had made a sacrifice of blood for his sin on the altar and washed himself in the laver could he pass through the first veil into the Holy Place.

When Jesus laid down His life for us and shed His blood on the Cross, He atoned for, or paid for, our sin forever, and His shed blood became a flowing fount, a holy laver that cleanses us from all sin. He became the living Way and the eternal Door into the Holy Place of God, where only priests could enter in. In that place, as priests of the Lord, we offer sacrifices of praise, worship, and adoration, guided and bathed by the light of His Word, and sustained by the bread of His Word and the fellowship of His broken Body, the Church.

GOING BEYOND THE VEIL

Then we pass through the veil into the Holy of Holies and stand before the ark of the covenant where the cherubim of gold hover over the mercy seat, the place of God's manifest presence. The mercy seat is barely visible through the sweetly fragrant smoke of the incense of our prayers, praise, and worship. Only the high priest could enter this place in the days before the cross, and then only once a year on the Day of Atonement.

The functions of the Old Testament priests foreshadow the greater reality God longs to see manifested in His priestly people today. The writer of Hebrews declares, *"But now He* [Jesus Christ] *has obtained a more excellent ministry, by as much as He is also the mediator of a better covenant, which has been enacted on better promises"* (Heb. 8:6). Then he carefully compares what I term "the glory of the former house" (the Jews' relationship to God through the law and animal sacrifice) to "the glory of the latter house" (the relationship of all men to God the Father through the blood of His Son, the Lamb of God, Jesus Christ).

Each function of the Aaronic priesthood represents a truth about man's relationship with God that we need to understand in the light of the cross:

1. In the Old Testament, only the high priest could enter the place of God's "residence" and have fellowship with Him. Under the new covenant executed by the death of Jesus Christ, *every believer is a priest.*

2. The priests of old knew God ritually, and in a relationship that was bound in fear without a revelation of love. Today, every believer can know God intimately and personally in a relationship marked by love, mercy, and grace.

3. The seemingly endless sacrifices of the old covenant had to be repeated each time the priest entered the tabernacle. Today, we have ready access to God anytime and all the time through the blood of Jesus, who paid the debt for our sin once and for all. Our sins are covered by His blood, and He has set us aside for Himself (sanctified us) as His prized possession, His Bride.

4. The descendants of Abraham knew God as the invisible Spirit who lived in a tent (and for a short time, in a stone house). Today, God has fulfilled His promise and He no longer resides in a tent. He lives

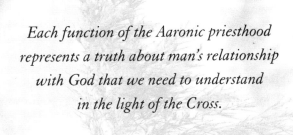

Each function of the Aaronic priesthood
represents a truth about man's relationship
with God that we need to understand
in the light of the Cross.

among men, instead, dwelling in our hearts in the person of the Holy Spirit. This same Spirit reveals God to every believer on a personal level, and we have intimate fellowship with God as a result.

The priestly functions of the Old Testament point us to our duties as the children of God in the New Testament. We now have been made priests and kings in the line of the Messiah as sons and daughters of God. However, our priesthood still includes the instruments of the Cross and an altar of sacrifice, just as it was for our Lord!

> *And He was saying to them all, "If anyone wishes to come after Me,* **he must deny himself, and take up his cross daily and follow Me.** *For whoever wishes to save his life will lose it, but whoever loses his life for My sake, he is the one who will save it"* (Luke 9:23-24).

> *Therefore I urge you, brethren, by the mercies of God,* **to present your bodies a living and holy sacrifice,** *acceptable to God, which is your spiritual service of worship. And do not be conformed to this world, but* **be transformed** *by the renewing of your mind, so that you may prove what the will of God is, that which is good and acceptable and perfect* (Romans 12:1-2).

God intended all along to form for Himself a Kingdom of priests and kings. He has always longed to fellowship with us at the altar of incense. Now He longs to call us closer, beyond the veil of separation, so He can meet and commune with us in the Most Holy Place of His manifest presence. So you see, the Aaronic priesthood of the Old Testament was just a shadow of what God really longed to do once the Sacrificed Lamb completed His mission of redemption.

Types and shadows or not, certain aspects of the priesthood of old were nevertheless ordained to carry over into our day. In Leviticus 16, God gave Moses very detailed instructions about the laws of atonement and the priestly progression into God's presence, and they contain something you and I need to understand in our day:

> *He shall take a firepan full of coals of fire from upon the altar before the Lord and two handfuls of finely ground sweet incense, and bring it inside the veil. He shall put the incense on the fire before the Lord, that the cloud of incense may cover the mercy seat that is on the ark of the testimony, otherwise he will die* (Leviticus 16:12-13).

> *Command the sons of Israel that they bring to you clear oil from beaten olives for the light, to make a lamp burn continually. Outside the veil of testimony in the tent of meeting, Aaron shall keep it in order from evening to morning before the Lord continually; it shall be a perpetual statute throughout your generations* (Leviticus 24:2-3).

These ordinances for the Holy Place and the Most Holy Place speak of "perpetual statutes for all generations." Perpetual *still* means forever, even in our generation. Did God not mean what He said? But I thought we were under a new covenant. All things are new; the old has passed away. So what does God mean by "forever" in this context?

Out of the Shadows Into the Light

God no longer requires us to keep vigil over a fire in a tent or stone temple, but the reality revealed in the principle remains perpetual. The sacrifices we should offer to the Lord as priests and kings include sacrifices of thanksgiving, praise, worship, unceasing prayer, and the service of intercession. That is why it is necessary for God to issue a call to intercession as a vital part of any effort to restore the priesthood of all believers to His Church. There is no way around it: Every priest of God is called and anointed to pray and intercede. A prayerless priest isn't a priest. Just as the

52

prayers and intercession of Aaron with the incense and fire from the altar saved the lives of thousands the day Korah rebelled in Numbers 16, so do our prayers and intercession make the difference for people today!

Did you realize that nowhere in the Scriptures is prayer, praise, worship, and intercession technically called a special spirit gift? It's not there— nowhere to be found! Do you know why? It's the right of every priest! God is an equal opportunity employer, and the ministry of prayer and praise is the job description of every authentic priest.

DEFINING OUR TERMS

According to *Merriam-Webster,* the word *intercede* means "to intervene between parties with a view to reconciling differences: mediate."[1] The Latin root words mean basically "to go between." As we noted in the previous chapter, the Hebrew word for intercession in the Messianic passage of Isaiah 59:16 is *paga*. It literally means to "strike the mark."

The importance of intercession in our day can't be overestimated, yet satan has been very successful in his attempts to convince Christians that prayer is mostly an exercise in futility. To action-oriented Americans in particular, prayer seems to be the silliest thing they could do in times of crisis, stress, or emergency. Jesus thought otherwise. Throughout the Gospels, we find Jesus disappearing to spend entire nights in fervent prayer before ministering to the

Every priest of God is called and anointed to pray and intercede. A prayerless priest isn't a priest. Just as the prayers and intercession of Aaron with the incense and fire from the altar saved the lives of thousands the day Korah rebelled in Numbers 16, so do our prayers and intercession make the difference for people today!

masses the following day. He chose to spend His last night before the crucifixion in the garden of Gethsemane—praying.

THE POWER OF INCENSE

In our day, there are countless stories of supernatural intervention through the power of prayer and intercession.

Jackie Pullinger-To is a wonderful, radical, missionary stateswoman serving the Lord in Hong Kong. At the age of 19 she was overcome with a passion to serve God. Though she didn't know where it was going to be, she just offered herself up unconditionally to Him for His service. God told her to get on a particular boat, so she got on the boat, not knowing where it was taking her. She got off in Hong Kong and was taken to a place called the "Walled City." There she met a man who was a kingpin of the drug lords in the Walled City. He had a brother named Alie who was studying to be a Buddhist monk. Alie was also facing court charges as an alleged accomplice with seven other men in the murder of a rival drug lord.

Jackie began to visit this particular Hong Kong jail every week to minister and to testify to these men, and specifically to Alie. Four of the men came to the Lord almost immediately. But though Jackie visited the jail every day for nine months, testifying to Alie about Jesus through a thick glass partition, he was unmoved.

Alie wouldn't admit it, but he was very afraid of dying for a crime that he did not do. Week after week, Jackie Pullinger-To continued to minister to him. "I know that you are afraid, Alie. I know that you are terrified of death, but I want to tell you that there is a loving God. There is a God of justice who knows all things and He is a Father of mercy. And I have enlisted Christians from all across the world to pray and fast on every Wednesday for you, Alie." Although Alie heard and understood the things Jackie was saying, he still refused to come to the Lord because his heart was hard.

One day the governor of the jail and a jail attendant passed by Alie's cell and remarked to one another that they smelled something. They did not know what the strange fragrance was, but they thought it was some kind of delicate perfume with a fragrant odor. They began asking Alie questions about the fragrance, but Alie said, "What smell?" Perplexed, the two men asked other inmates about the smell, as the entire jail cell took on the fragrant odor of this strange perfume.

Finally, the governor of the jail sent authorities into Alie's cell. They searched his body and found nothing. When they sniffed the air around him, they nodded and said, "Yes, the smell is here." Yet Alie still smelled nothing. When the guards left, Alie began to ask himself, *What is that smell?* Then a little Word trickled down inside him. It was this simple message: "Oh, it is Wednesday!" Suddenly, he remembered Jackie's words. *He was smelling prayer!* He realized his entire jail cell was filled with the fragrant aroma of the prayers of the saints.

As Jackie continued to visit Alie, they talked of these things. One day Alie accepted Jesus as Jackie prayed for him through the glass partition. The Holy Spirit came upon him and Alie began to speak in another language. The time came for his court trial. Alie went before the judge, who released him without ever hearing the case!

THE FRAGRANCE OF PRAYER

Alie was saved because of the prayers offered to God on his behalf. So many prayers were directed at him in his tiny jail cell that the air was saturated with the sweet incense of intercession. When believers from all over the world began to exercise their priestly duties and offer the incense of intercession before the presence of the Lord, the air in that Hong Kong prison cell was so filled with prayer that even unbelievers could smell the fragrance! The fruit of that prayer was that Alie surrendered his life to Jesus. Is anyone smelling your prayers? Can anyone tell what day it is by the fragrance of your intercession?

The laws of God are immutable, including the natural laws of gravity. "What goes up must come down!" The law of gravity applies here. In the days of Aaron, the incense of prayer created a cloud as the fragrant smoke of the incense covered the mercy seat on the ark of the covenant. Then God would descend and distill His visible qualities in the midst of the cloud where He would commune with the high priest. The presence of God always descended *after* the fragrance of prayer ascended. In our day, an entire kingdom of priests has been authorized and commissioned to minister in God's presence, offering up unceasing prayer, praise, worship, and intercession for all men.

I have pondered all of these things in the light of Revelation 5:8, which opens a window for us into the operations and functions of the heavenly realm. John tells us that there is an altar in Heaven where the angels minister to the Lord continuously. One angel has a censer that must be similar to the fire pan of the Aaronic priests.

> *Another angel came and stood at the altar, holding a golden censer; and much incense was given to him, so that he might add it to the prayers of all the saints on the golden altar which was before the throne. And the smoke of the incense, with the prayers of the saints, went up before God out of the angel's hand. Then the angel took the censer and filled it with the fire of the altar, and threw it to the earth; and there followed peals of thunder and sounds and flashes of lightning and an earthquake* (Revelation 8:3-5).

The Bible says that the angel took the censer and filled it with fire from the altar mingled with incense. Beside this altar in Heaven, there is also a golden bowl filled with incense. What is incense? Revelation 5:8 tells us that this incense is the prayers of the saints. What is the Lord's response to the fragrance of the incense of our prayers rising before Him? He commands an angel to turn over that bowl and spill the prayers of the saints onto the fire of the altar! Then the angel takes the censer and fills it with fire from the altar and the incense of the prayers of the saints and casts the fire down from Heaven onto the earth.

As we have said before: *What goes up must come down.* When the prayers of the saints rise as incense before the throne of God, they are gathered into a golden bowl and burned again with the fire of the altar in the presence of the Most High God. This illustrates how our prayers are multiplied and savored by God before He responds by sending His fire to the earth as answered prayer. This is the multidirectional dimension of prayer. Remember, what goes up must come down.

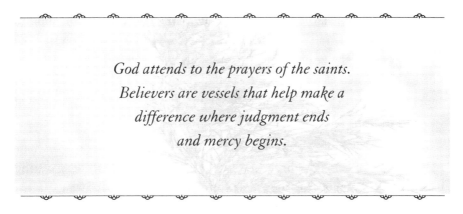

*God attends to the prayers of the saints.
Believers are vessels that help make a
difference where judgment ends
and mercy begins.*

WHERE WILL THE JUDGMENTS BE RELEASED?

The interesting thing is that the Bible doesn't say where on the earth these judgments will be released. Why is that? Before releasing judgment, God always attends first to the golden bowl, the prayers of the saints. He first listens to the priests who are ministering in the tabernacle at the altar of incense, which is the priestly act of intercession. Believers are vessels that help make a difference where judgment ends and mercy begins.

God has chosen to raise up an entire Kingdom of intercessory priests like Abraham (who interceded for Lot and the cities of Sodom and Gomorrah), Moses (who stood between God's wrath and the Israelites repeatedly), Job (who interceded for his friends and was himself healed and restored), Esther (the peasant who became queen and risked death to intercede for the salvation of her entire nation), and Daniel (whose intercession for his nation extended beyond his own time into the last days before the final return of the Messiah). Even more remarkable is the fact that God wants us to model our priesthood after the continual ministry of our Great High Priest, Jesus Christ, who *"is able also to save them to the uttermost that come unto God by Him, seeing He ever liveth to make intercession for them"* (Heb. 7:25 KJV).

EXPOSING THE ENEMY'S LIES

Let me say this for the benefit of everyone who has unknowingly bought the enemy's desperate lies about the supposed uselessness of prayer: **Prayer works. Prayer is powerful. Prayer is one of our most deadly and effective weapons for destroying the works of the enemy. Prayer is God's lifeline to the**

hurting, the wounded, the weak, and the dying. But He expects you and I to throw out His rope of life in the name of His Son, Jesus. Intercession isn't the preoccupation of the zealous few; it is the calling and destiny of the Chosen people, of every blood-washed child of God. If you call Jesus Christ your Savior and Lord, then He calls you intercessor and priest, and today He is calling you to your knees.

A few years ago, I was traveling in the middle of the night on a six-hour train trip from Heidelberg to Rosenheim, Germany. I tried to sleep during that trip, but I kept hearing the gentle voice of the Holy Spirit speak to me. I knew that He was speaking to me as an individual, but He was also voicing His burden for the many-membered people to come forth.

I repeatedly heard that dear Dove utter a piercing, relentless plea: "Where are My Daniels? Where are My Esthers? Where are My Deborahs? And where are My Josephs?"

Jesus Christ has made you and I to be kings and priests unto God. Now I declare to you under the same prophetic anointing that inspired Mordecai when he told his young cousin and ward, Esther, *"And who knows whether you have not **attained royalty for such a time as this?**"* (Esther 4:14b). For such a task as this were you apprehended, and for this purpose He brought you forth. As a Christlike one, you also are named deliverer, kinsman redeemer, healer, and restorer of the breach. Will you arise and be one of His radical revolutionaries? Will you say "Yes, Lord!" and be the *answer* to the Great Intercessor's plea?

By the grace of God, I want to be a New Testament priestly intercessor! I want the fragrance of prayer to emanate from my life and influence the activity of heaven. I volunteer to be one of your Daniels, Esthers, Deborahs and Josephs for this generation. Give me the spirit of grace and supplication so that Heaven will respond when I pray for revival's sake! Amen!

ENDNOTE

1. *Merriam-Webster's Collegiate Dictionary, 10th Edition* (Springfield, MA: Merriam-Webster, Incorporated, 1994), 609.

CHAPTER 4

Restoring the Art of Pleading Your Case

"It is the habit of faith, when she is praying, to use pleas. Mere prayer sayers, who do not pray at all, forget to argue with God; but those who would prevail bring forth their reasons and their strong arguments...."

—Charles H. Spurgeon

Unthinkable! How could you presume to argue with God? It is not presumption to obey the Word of God, nor is it presumption to remind God of His mighty works and unmatched power. God is pleased each and every time we come before His throne as we are whispering, reciting, declaring, and pleading for the speedy fulfillment of His unfailing promises in Jesus' name. He is glorified when His children humbly urge and entreat Him to rise in His power on behalf of those in need—when they recite the countless ways He has delivered in the past, is redeeming in the present, and will overcome in the days to come.

Presumption presumes to act on authority that it does not have or has not been given; obedience only acts on the authority of another or upon the authority that it has been given by a higher authority. We have been given incredible "royal court" privileges and authority by our Lord, Jesus Christ. He has personally made each of us priests and kings with right of entry to the very throne of God. Even a casual glance at the instructions of Jesus concerning the prevailing prayer of the persistent widow who pestered the unrighteous judge to take action in Luke 18:1-8 should be a warning that there is more to this "pleading prayer" than most people believe.

> *"Even though I do not fear God nor respect man, yet because this widow bothers me, I will give her legal protection, otherwise by continually coming she will wear me out."* And the Lord said, *"Hear what the unrighteous judge said; now,* **will not God bring about justice for His elect who cry to Him day and night,** *and will He delay long over them? I tell you that He will bring about justice for them quickly. However, when the Son of Man comes, will He find faith on the earth?"*
> (Luke 18:4b-8)

Isaiah, the prophet, battled with an unrepentant and even defiant nation of Israelites who refused to acknowledge sin or abandon its idols even in the face of defeat, bondage, and literal slavery to other nations. Then God issued a challenge to His creation through the prophet that reveals the heart of God toward us—even when we are in sin and trying to justify our rebellion.

> *Put* **Me** *in* **remembrance**: *let us* **plead** *together:* **declare** *thou, that thou mayest be justified* (Isaiah 43:26 KJV).

> *Put* **Me** *in* **remembrance**; *let us* **argue** *our case together,* **state** *your cause, that you may be proved right* (Isaiah 43:26).

> *Oh,* **remind** *Me of this promise of forgiveness, for we must* **talk** *about your sins.* **Plead** *your case for My forgiving you* (Isaiah 43:26 TLB).

This verse reveals the "broad shoulders of God," who is so powerful and confident that He can "afford" to listen the arguments of mankind—even those of angry or disillusioned people who often step far beyond the bounds of wisdom in their complaints to God. He especially delights in the humble but confident prayers of His kings and priests who come to His court in the name and company of His Son, Jesus Christ, approaching Him on the basis of His Word.

DEFINING THE TERMS

This clear biblical precedent establishes the fact that we have God's permission and invitation to plead our case and make appeals in the courts of Heaven before our great Judge and God. The dictionary definition of *plead* is "1: to argue a case or cause in a court of law; 2: to make an allegation in an action or other legal proceeding," and a definition for *plea* is "an earnest entreaty."[1]

The Hebrew word translated as "plead" in Isaiah's declaration is *shaphat*. It means "to judge, to pronounce sentence, to vindicate, to punish, or to litigate.[2] The Hebrew word translated as "declare" or "state your cause" is *caphar*, which means "to score with a mark as a tally or record, to inscribe, and also to enumerate; to recount, to number."[3]

These definitions taken together paint a clear picture of a judicial setting described in purely judicial terminology: to argue the case as in a court of law, to pronounce sentence, to punish, to litigate. This reinforces my conviction that for us to succeed as intercessors, we must have a revelation of God Almighty as the Judge of all flesh. We are privileged to "practice before the bar" under the authority and invitation of our Judge Advocate, Jesus Christ.

Recently I was given a dream with my next intercessory commission contained within. I was told in the vivid dream, "You have been used to redig the wells of the watch of the Lord, prophetic intercession, crisis intervention and the contemplative watch. But now I call you to pioneer Judicial Intercession. I call you to learn and release courtroom hearings before my throne where the intercessor works with my son as the advocate lawyer." I woke up from this experience and my heart said, "Yes, Lord!" It is time for us to come boldly before His throne to receive our just reward!

ASSISTING THE ADVOCATE

At our new birth, He was our defense attorney. As intercessors of the Lamb, we serve as assistant advocates of the Kingdom, charged with defending the King's people and prosecuting the King's enemies in the spirit realm (the adversary and his rebellious followers). Each time we come before the "bench" of the Judge of all, our Chief Advocate comes alongside and takes us by the arm to formally present us before the Judge and enumerate the legal credentials that He has delegated to us. We literally "practice before the bar" as assistant advocates sent from His high office as First Born, the Lamb of God, Chief Intercessor, and Chief Advocate of the redeemed.

The writer of Hebrews carefully painted a picture to contrast the difference between man's approach to the Judge before the cross and after the cross. The difference is absolutely crucial:

As intercessors of the Lamb, we serve as assistant advocates of the Kingdom, charged with defending the King's people and prosecuting the King's enemies in the spirit realm (the adversary and his rebellious followers).

For you have not come to a mountain that can be touched and to a blazing fire, and to darkness and gloom and whirlwind, and to the blast of a trumpet and the sound of words which sound was such that those who heard begged that no further word should be spoken to them. For they could not bear the command, "If even a beast touches the mountain, it will be stoned." And so terrible was the sight, that Moses said, "I am full of fear and trembling" (Hebrews 12:18-21).

Compare the Old Covenant picture of fear and dread with our place of entry under the New Covenant of the blood of the Lamb:

But you have come to Mount Zion and to the city of the living God, the heavenly Jerusalem, and to myriads of angels, to the general assembly

> *and church of the firstborn who are enrolled in Heaven, and to God, the Judge of all, and to the spirits of the righteous made perfect, and to Jesus, the mediator of a new covenant, and to the sprinkled blood, which speaks better than the blood of Abel* (Hebrews 12:22-24).

The Book of Hebrews describes the dwelling place of God and the beings who dwell there with Him. We are reassured as we realize that when we step before the bench of this Judge, we will be in the company of the worshiping angels and familiar people like Moses; Aaron; Hur; Isaiah; Deborah; Paul; Barnabas; Simon of Cyrene; Mary, the mother of Jesus; Peter, the fisherman-made-apostle; Corrie ten Boom; Teresa of Avila; Paul Billheimer; C.S. Lewis; Nikolaus Ludwig von Zinzendorf; and the Wesley brothers. Do you sense that you would be at home in this place?

Best of all, as we come before the Judge of all to plead our intercessory case, we come to the Advocate, the Merciful One, Jesus Christ the mediator, whose sprinkled blood continually cries out, "Mercy," before the Judge (while the blood of Abel could only cry, "Vengeance!").

When you persistently bring your pleas before the Judge of all in the courtroom of Heaven, the Lord looks upon it as faith. The process of presenting your case and arguments pleases God, and it also helps you understand the need more completely. It moves you in compassion, strengthens your determination, and arms you with a greater depth of holy hunger.

In the first chapter of Isaiah's prophetic book, God declares, *"Come now, and let us reason together..."* (Isa. 1:18). This is an invitation to a court hearing where God is pleased to hear our requests, petitions, and pleas. Job openly longed for such a place:

> *Oh that I knew where I might find Him, that I might come to His seat! I would present my case before Him and fill my mouth with arguments. I would learn the words which He would answer, and perceive what He would say to me* (Job 23:3-5).

I have received a great deal of inspiration and instruction from Wesley Duewel's book titled, *Mighty Prevailing Prayer*. He quotes Charles Spurgeon's comments on intercession in his book: "It is the habit of faith, when she is praying, to use pleas. Mere prayer sayers, who do not pray at all, forget to argue with God; but those who would prevail bring forth their reasons and their strong arguments...Faith's act of wrestling is to plead with God and say with holy boldness, 'Let it be thus and thus for these reasons.'" Spurgeon preached, "The man who has his mouth full of arguments in prayers shall soon have his mouth full of benedictions in answered prayer."[4]   Wesley Duewel outlines a blueprint for reciting our case before God:

> This holy argumentation with God is not done in a negative, complaining spirit. It is the expression not of a critical heart but of a heart burning with love for God, for His name, and for His glory. This holy debate with God is a passionate presentation to God of the many reasons why it will be in harmony with His nature, His righteous government, and the history of His holy intervention on behalf of His people.
>
> You do not plead like a negative, legal adversary in the presence of God the holy judge. Rather, you plead in the form of a well-prepared brief, prepared by a legal advocate in behalf of a need and for the welfare of the kingdom. At times you are, as it were, petitioning God's court for an injunction against satan to stop his harassment. The Holy Spirit guides you in the preparation and wording of your prayer argument.[5]

DOING YOUR HOMEWORK!

Effective intercession begins with knowledge and understanding. Do your homework so you will know God's promises. Understand why the promises haven't been fulfilled in specific situations (when possible). Know why society or a particular group has failed. Understand every condition God requires before His various promises are fulfilled. Then commune with Jesus and get His heart on the matter. Let the Holy Spirit be your guide as you present holy argumentation before the righteous Judge of all the living. As you enter His presence, remember that many have come here before you. Thousands of years ago, the prophet Jeremiah and Joshua each ventured to this place of intercession:

Although our iniquities testify against us, O Lord, act for Your name's sake!... Do not despise us, for Your own name's sake; do not disgrace the throne of Your glory; remember and do not annul Your covenant with us (Jeremiah 14:7,21).

Joshua pleaded with God to help Israel, asking, *"What will You do for Your own name's sake?"* (see Josh. 7:9b).

IN THE FOOTSTEPS OF ABRAHAM

One of the first great intercessors in the Bible was Abraham, and his most famous intercessory prayer was for one of the most sinful places in the ancient world! Sodom and Gomorrah have become synonymous with sin, sexual debauchery, and sodomy, yet the great patriarch of Israel, the "father of faith," interceded passionately that those twin cities of sin be spared! I believe it was this kind of compassion that led God to say, *"Shall I hide from Abraham what I am about to do?"* (Gen. 18:17).

When God told Abraham that He planned to destroy Sodom and Gomorrah, the patriarch asked God if He planned to destroy the righteous people along with the wicked. Abraham then made the counterproposal, *"Will You indeed sweep it away and not spare the place for the sake of the fifty righteous who are in it?"* (Gen. 18:24b) When God agrees to relent if 50 righteous people were found, Abraham persisted to drive the numbers lower, knowing only Lot and his family could possibly qualify. The patriarch whittled the number down to 20, and in verse 32 he reached a pivotal place that is important for us to see. Abraham said, *"Oh may the Lord not be angry, and I shall speak only this once; suppose ten are found there?"* (Gen. 18:32).

God agrees to Abraham's request, but this passage caused us to wonder, *What if Abraham hadn't stopped at ten?* God definitely showed no signs of being angry with Abraham over his persistent intercession and pleading on behalf of Sodom and Gomorrah. In fact, I believe God liked it. I believe Abraham could have gone even lower. (But then again I wasn't there and I

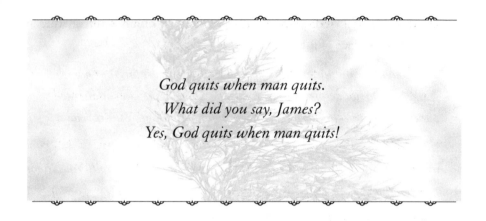

God quits when man quits.
What did you say, James?
Yes, God quits when man quits!

certainly don't have all the facts at hand.) However, this incident illustrates one of the fundamental laws governing the relationship between God and man: God quits when man quits. What did you say, James? Yes, God quits when man quits!

BIBLICAL DEFINITIONS

There are four biblical definitions of an intercessor that help paint a clear picture of our general calling as priestly intercessors and will bring everything else we study into proper perspective.

An intercessor is one who:

1. **Reminds the Lord of promises and appointments not yet met and fulfilled.**

   On your walls, O Jerusalem, I have appointed watchmen; all day and all night they will never keep silent. You who **remind the Lord***, take no rest for yourselves; and give Him no rest until He establishes and makes Jerusalem a praise in the earth* (Isaiah 62:6-7).

2. **Takes up the case of justice before God on behalf of another.**

   Yes, truth is lacking; and he who turns aside from evil makes himself a prey. Now the Lord saw, and it was displeasing in His sight that there was no justice. And He saw that there was no man, and was astonished that there was no one to intercede (Isaiah 59:15-16a).

3. **Makes up the hedge, and builds up the wall of protection in time of battle.**

O Israel, your prophets have been like foxes among ruins. You have not gone up into the breaches, nor did you build the wall around the house of Israel to stand in the battle on the day of the Lord (Ezekiel 13:4-5).

4. **Stands in the gap between God's righteous judgment, which is due, and the need for mercy on the people's behalf.**

*"And I searched for a man among them who should **build up the wall** and **stand in the gap** before Me for the land, that I should not destroy it; but I found no one. Thus I have poured out My indignation on them; I have consumed them with the fire of My wrath; their way I have brought upon their heads," declares the Lord God* (Ezekiel 22:30-31).

RESPONDING TO HIS PROMISES

Priestly intercessors deal with two kinds of promises: the promises recorded in the Word of God that are yet to be fulfilled or are ongoing promises available to every believer by faith; and prophetic promises given to us in our day that are true, but are yet to be fulfilled (see 1 Tim. 1:18-19).

God tells us in the Book of Jeremiah that He is watching over His Word to perform it (see Jer. 1:12). That means the most valid and effective way to present our case before God is to rehearse and respectfully remind Him of His unchanging Word. When we rehearse a promise from our faithful God, *He requires Himself* to watch over that Word to perform it. But this entreaty only can be done with the purest of motives from hearts that are clean before God. Even then, we are only authorized to "argue" or present our case for those things and petitions that (1) are in accordance with God's will; (2) extend His Kingdom; and (3) glorify His name.

Wesley Duewel lists seven bases of appeal for intercessory prayer in his book, *Mighty Prevailing Prayer*. These points provide a powerful platform of knowledge for anointed and effective intercession. It is not enough to get inspired and to have sincerity when we pray. We need to understand our God-given rights and privileges, and we need to understand our limitations and boundaries. That way, we can stand before the Judge in confidence. We will know that we are not merely trying to "twist the arm of God" to get Him to do something that He does not want to do. Quite to the contrary, we are called to ask Him to do what He wants to do for us! What a deal!

A. Plead the Honor and Glory of God's Name

1. God saved Israel at the Red Sea for His name's sake *"that He might make His power known"* (Ps. 106:8).

2. Samuel prayed for the sake of God's own name (see 2 Sam. 7:26).

3. David, knowing the God-given responsibility kingship placed upon him, prayed for guidance (see Ps. 23:3; 31:3), and for help (see Ps. 109:21; 143:11), and for God's name's sake.

4. Asaph prayed for God to help Israel *"for the glory of Your name"* (Ps. 79:9a).

B. Plead God's Relationships to Us

1. God is our *Creator* and we are the work of His hands (see Job 10:3,8-9; 14:15; Ps. 119:73).

2. God is our *Helper* (see Ps. 33:20; 40:17; 63:7), our ever-present help (see Ps. 46:1).

3. God is our *Redeemer* (see Ps. 19:14; Isa. 41:14; 54:5). He will have compassion on us because He is our Redeemer (see Isa. 54:8; 63:16).

4. God is our *Father* (see Isa. 64:8; Mal. 3:17; Rom. 8:15), and we are privileged to cry out as children to their father, *"Abba* [Daddy]! *Father!"* (Rom. 8:15; Gal. 4:6).

   Since He is our Creator, Helper, Redeemer, and Father, we can make our plea to Him for protection and provision for all He has created and redeemed.

C. Plead God's Attributes

1. Plead God's *righteousness* as Nehemiah did (see Neh. 9:33). Christ speeds the cause of the righteous (see Isa. 16:5).

2. Plead on the basis of God's *faithfulness* as Ethan did in Psalm 89, where he makes his holy plea according to God's faithfulness six times.

3. Plead on the basis of His *mercy and love.* Join Moses (see Deut. 9:18), David (see Ps. 4:1; 27:7; 30:10; 86:6,15-16), and Daniel and the three Hebrew children (see Dan. 2:18).

4. Charles Spurgeon said, "We shall find every attribute of God Most High to be, as it were, a great battering ram with which we may open the gates of heaven."

D. Plead the Sorrows and Needs of God's People

1. David was one who took upon himself the suffering of his people. He even wept for the suffering of his enemies (see Ps. 35:11-13). Nehemiah and Daniel, in particular, also used this plea greatly as they vicariously identified themselves with the sufferings of the people.

2. Jeremiah, perhaps more than others, used this form of plea as he prevailed for his people. He pleads for God to look and see the sufferings (see Lam. 2:20), and to remember, look, and see (see Lam. 5:1). In great detail he lists for God all the sufferings of the people. He does not try to justify his people, for he knows how deserving they are of God's judgment.

    Let me give you a contemporary example: I have ministered in the Caribbean nation of Haiti 14 different times. It is the poorest country in the western hemisphere, and it is one of the poorest nations in the world. The adult per capita income before the recent food embargo was $300 a year. Among adult males in the capital city of Port-au-Prince, the unemployment rate has been 80 percent! Disease is rampant. If you go into nearby suburbs like the city of Solle, conditions are horrendous with no sanitation facilities or bathrooms. (I didn't even see an outhouse when I walked the streets at Solle.) In the 1800s, Haiti was called "the pearl of the Antilles," and Port-au-Prince was supposedly named for the Prince of Peace. But the people so desperately wanted their independence from the domination of France that they dedicated the nation to satan, believing he would give them power to be free.

Well, they got their freedom from France, but they received enslavement to the dark powers driving their voodoo religion. At the same time, these are some of the most lovely people I have ever met. My heart aches to again see the many wonderful God-fearing believers I've met in that nation. The indigenous church is arising, and my prayer for this nation that was dedicated to darkness is this: "Father, bring these precious people to repentance, and break the bondage of satan that binds them. Restore them into their ancient godly heritage and make them once again the pearl of the Antilles. Let God arise and His enemies be scattered!"

E. Plead the Past Answers to Prayer

1. David reminded God of His past mercy: *"Thou hast been my help"* (Ps. 27:9b). *"O God, Thou hast taught me...even when I am old and gray, O God do not forsake me"* (Ps. 71:17-18a). A number of psalms remind God and the people in detail of His past mercies (see Ps. 78; 85:1-7; 105; 106; and 136).

2. Like David, you can present pleading arguments for new mercies on the basis of the history of all He previously has done. But the task is yet unfinished. God has invested too much to stop now. Plead for God's continuing mercy and power to be renewed to bring the final victory.

3. What has God done for you? How have your prayers been answered in the past? Just begin to praise and thank the Lord for the answers of the past, and renewed faith will arise within you for your plea-saying of today.

F. Plead the Word and the Promises of God

1. David cried to God reverently, humbly, and lovingly, yet with holy insistence. He pressed for fulfillment of God's promise,

"Do as You have spoken. Let Your name be established and mag-nified forever…therefore Your servant has found courage to pray before You. Now, O Lord, You are God, and have promised this good thing to Your servant" (1 Chron. 17:23-26).

2.   Solomon prayed the same way. He held God to the promises that He had made to David, his father: *"…O Lord, the God of Israel, there is no god like You in heaven or on earth, keeping covenant and showing lovingkindness to Your servants who walk before You with all their heart; who has kept with Your servant David, my father, that which You have promised him; indeed, You have spoken with Your mouth, and have fulfilled it with Your hand, as it is this day. Now therefore, O Lord, the God of Israel, keep with Your servant David, my father, that which You have promised him, saying, 'You shall not lack a man to sit on the throne of Israel, if only your sons take heed to their way, to walk in My law as you have walked before Me.' Now therefore, O Lord, the God of Israel, let Your word be confirmed which You have spoken to Your servant David"* (2 Chron. 6:14-17). This was no mincing of words. God had spoken. Now Solomon insisted that God fulfill His Word.

For 11 years I was a part of the leadership team of a church that prepared the ground for the International House of Prayer in Kansas City, Missouri. In that time, I had the awe-some privilege of participating in countless numbers of prayer gatherings led under the inspiration of the senior leader, Mike Bickle. Meeting by meeting, day by day, and month by month, Mike and scores of "faceless people" would take their stand before God and remind Him of His Word. Praying the prayers of the Bible, turning Scripture portions into intercession, pleading promises of this grand Book back to God. This ancient art is intercession in one of its purest forms.

G. Plead the Blood of Jesus

1. Perhaps the greatest, most powerful, most answerable plea of all is the blood of Jesus. No more prevailing argument can we bring before God than the sufferings, blood, and death of His Son. We have no merit of our own. We do not prevail by techniques or past experience. No prayer "know-how" prevails. It is only through the blood of Jesus.

2. Bring before the Father the wounds of Jesus. Remind the Father of the agony of Gethsemane. Recall to the Father the strong cries of the Son of God as He prevailed for our world and for our salvation. Remind the Father of earth's darkest hour on Calvary, as

> *The name of Jesus and the blood of Jesus—glory in them, stake your all on them, and use them to the glory of God and the routing of satan. Let there be a generation of people arise who are consumed with this passion, with this vision of the blood of Jesus.*

the Son triumphed alone for you and me. Shout to Heaven again Christ's triumphant cry, "It is finished!" Plead the Cross. Plead His wounds over and over again.

3. Pray until you have the assurance of God's will. Pray until you have been given by the Spirit a vision of what God longs to do, needs to do, and waits to do. Pray until you are gripped by the authority of the name of Jesus. Then plead the blood of Jesus. The name of Jesus and the blood of Jesus—glory in them, stake your all on them, and use them to the glory of God and the routing of satan. Let there be a generation of people arise

who are consumed with this passion, with this vision of the blood of Jesus.

THE POWER OF THE BLOOD!

Over the past 30-plus years my wife and I have had the privilege of knowing Mahesh and Bonnie Chavda of All Nations Church in Charlotte, North Carolina. Mahesh has traveled the globe, and through the authentic healing ministry of Jesus Christ, through our dear humble brother, he has seen every healing listed in the New Testament, including the dead being raised.

One time, when Mahesh was ministering in Zaire, Africa, he stood before a multitude of over 100,000 people. The Holy Spirit spoke to him to conduct a mass deliverance service. Mahesh answered back, "But Lord, where are my helpers?"

Our persistent, great God responded, "I am thy Helper! Know this— one drop of the blood of My Son, Jesus, is more powerful than all the kingdom of darkness." With this powerful revelation, Mahesh proceeded, and thousands were cleansed, healed, and delivered that day.

Let us join in with evangelist Reinhard Bonnke as he issues a proclamation for a "blood-washed Africa!" Let us arise and join the prayers of Spurgeon, Moody, Chavda, and others. Let's declare what the blood of Jesus, our Messiah, has accomplished for us.

COME, LET US ARGUE TOGETHER

What is the final outcome? What will be the score at the end of such a day? Our result is spelled out by the prophet Isaiah who declared by God's Spirit: *"Put Me in remembrance, let us argue our case together; state your cause, that you may be proved right"* (Isa. 43:26).[6]

There is a Kingdom to expand and extend. There are blood-washed believers to uplift and protect in prayer. There are millions of lost and dying people desperately in need of the Savior. There are evil forces to bind and dispel through the weapons of divine warfare. It is time to prepare a court brief, to devise arguments of divine value and merit based on the ancient promises of our Eternal God. Are you prepared to approach the bench of the Most High as an advocate of His people, His purposes, and His glory? Gather your case, check your heart, and fall to your knees. The court of the Righteous Judge is always convened and ready to hear your pleas. What case are you ready to bring?

I choose to be a tenacious intercessor! Make me bold and full of faith to plead the promises of God before a judicial courtroom hearing. But faith, my prayers shall pierce this present darkness and unlock the promises of God for my generation. Lay hold of me! Possess me for the purposes of God in this chosen generation!

(I strongly recommend to you Wesley Duewel's excellent book, *Mighty Prevailing Prayer*. The late Leonard Ravenhill called it "the encyclopedia on prayer." I believe it. Much of what I have presented to you on the subject of "pleading your case" was inspired by, or derived from, the material in *Mighty Prevailing Prayer*. Also for more on the subject of prophetic intercession, see my inspirational book *The Prophetic Intercessor*.)[6]

ENDNOTES

1. *Merriam-Webster's Collegiate Dictionary, 10th Edition,* 893.

2. James Strong, *Strong's Exhaustive Concordance of the Bible* (Peabody, MA: Hendrickson Publishers, n.d.), **plead** (#5608).

3. Strong's, **declare** (#5608).

4. Wesley Duewel, *Mighty Prevailing Prayer* (Grand Rapids, MI: Francis Asbury Press, 1990).

5. Duewel, *Mighty Prevailing*.

6. Duewel, *Mighty Prevailing*.

CHAPTER 5

Restoring the Watch of the Lord

"I will restore the ancient tools of the Watch of the Lord that have been used and will be used again to change the expression of Christianity across the face of the earth."

—*June 1991*

This prophetic word came to me in the middle of the night on the Kansas plains. I had brought 30 people with me to that remote area for a prayer retreat at a country lodge. We were praying around the clock in prayer teams for "hour watches" or prayer periods, modeled after military sentry patterns. Our focus was not on fellowship or even a prayer list; we were there to seek God's face. As usual, I had chosen the 2:00-to-3:00 A.M. time slot because the Lord had been waking me up at that time virtually two or three times a week for more than a decade.

As I waited on the Lord, I suddenly saw a picture of an old farm implement, the kind of plow that used to be drawn by horses. When I asked the Lord what it was, the Holy Spirit said, "These are the ancient tools." When

I asked what these were, the response was immediate: "The *Watch of the Lord* is the ancient tool." Now that phrase went deep inside of me and stuck.

As I continued to wait before the Lord in that quiet, far-removed place, I saw the tool again and the Lord said, "I will restore the ancient tool of the Watch of the Lord. It has been used and will be used again to change the expression of Christianity across the face of the earth." It sounded very similar to something the Lord said to my friend, Pastor Mike Bickle, when he was in Cairo, Egypt, in 1982. The Lord spoke to him about a move of the Spirit that was coming. He said, "I will change the understanding and the expression of Christianity across the face of the earth in one generation."

I was already familiar with the concept of "watching in prayer" in the Old and the New Testaments (sorry to say, it is sorely missing from the life of the Church at large). This clear word of the Lord given under the starry skies of Kansas lit a fire under me that ultimately propelled me into the borderland of ancient Saxony, the ancient site of the Moravian prayer watch at Herrnhut that I described earlier.

Few English-speaking people use the term "Watch of the Lord" in our day. Books on prayer seldom discuss it. Yet the importance of the Watch of the Lord, or of watching in prayer, is very important to the plans and order of God. Jesus commanded us to "watch" with Him in several Gospel accounts, particularly in the time called "the last days."

Much has been taught about "the last days" by teachers in Evangelical and Pentecostal/Charismatic circles. But exceptionally little has been taught about the *biblical response* of God's people to the last days. I made a comparative study of the verbs Jesus used in Matthew 24, Mark 13, and Luke 21, where He described how we should respond when we see earthquakes, famines, wars and rumors of wars, and so on. Here is a summary of these responses:

See Matthew 24 (NIV):

"Watch out that no one deceives you" (verse 4).

"See to it that you are not alarmed" (verse 6).

"[Stand] firm to the end" (verse 13).

"Keep watch" (verse 42).

See Mark 13 (NIV):

"Watch out that no one deceives you" (verse 5).

"Do not be alarmed" (verse 7).

"Be on your guard" (verse 9).

"Do not worry" (verse 11).

"[Stand] firm" (verse 13).

"Be on your guard" (verse 23).

"Be on guard! Be alert" (verse 33).

"Keep watch" (verse 35).

"Watch [out]" (verse 37).

See Luke 21 (NIV):

"Watch out that you are not deceived" (verse 8).

"Do not be frightened" (verse 9).

"[Stand] firm" (verse 19).

"Stand up and lift up your heads" (verse 28).

"Be careful" (verse 34).

"Be always on the watch, and pray" (verse 36).

All of these statements can be summarized in three main phrases: "Do not be afraid" (mentioned four times), "Stand firm" (mentioned four times), and "Watch." Jesus used this key word, "watch," 11 times—almost three times more than any other admonition! Once again, you can hear His voice saying to the Church, "The key I give you is 'watch.' " In Matthew 18:19-20, He gave us the keys of the Kingdom, and they have to do with prayer:

> *Again I say to you, that if two of you agree on earth about anything that they may ask, it shall be done for them by My Father who is in Heaven. For where two or three have gathered together in My name, there I am in their midst* (Matthew 18:19-20).

Jesus wants groups of two or three people to gather in His name and ask in symphony or harmony. (The Greek word translated "agree" is *sumphoneo*, or "harmonious.") This is the heart of the "watch of the Lord." I know it's profound, but you don't need a doctorate in theology or linguistics to understand it.

The Greek word for "watch" in these verses is *gregoreuo*, and it means "to be vigilant, wake, to be watchful."[1] A watchman on the wall does many things. He carefully watches what is happening and alerts the community when good ambassadors approach the city. The guardsman then will open the gates and lower the bridge so the ambassadors may enter. A watchman also warns the city far in advance when an enemy approaches. He sounds an alarm to awaken the people because he knows "to forewarn them is to alert and arm them." Then they quickly can rally to take their stand on the wall against the enemy before he wrongfully tries to enter into the city.

PUTTING OUT THE WELCOME MAT

We must watch for the good things and good messengers God sends to His people. We must watch for the gifted ones and the coming of the Lord's presence. We should alert the people to roll out the welcome mat, saying, "Come, come, come, come! Angels of healing, you are welcome here. Spirit of the Lord, You are welcome here. Gifts of the Spirit, you are welcome here. Spirit of conviction of sin, righteousness, and judgment come; You are welcome here. Come, come, come, come!" We should roll out the red carpet to the name and the blood of Jesus, and say, "Come!"

We are supposed to watch to see what the Lord is saying and doing. And we should look at what the enemy's plans could be. Paul warned us not to be ignorant concerning the devil's schemes (see 2 Cor. 2:11). God wants to tip us off beforehand to cut off, postpone, delay, or even entirely dismantle the works of the enemy and frustrate his plans for evil.

But as watchers on the wall of the Lord, we go far beyond any dictionary definition. God wants us to look into the mirror of His great Word and discern those things that He has said that He wants to do. Then we are supposed to remind Him of those things that He wants to do, and He is, at the same time, waiting for us to ask Him to do them. Why? Because He has given us that little key called the "prayer of agreement."

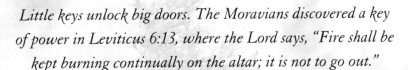

Little keys unlock big doors. The Moravians discovered a key of power in Leviticus 6:13, where the Lord says, "Fire shall be kept burning continually on the altar; it is not to go out."

They believed the New Covenant fire on the altar was prayer, and they acted on God's challenge. The Moravians actually managed to change the world with that little key.

Little keys unlock big doors. The Moravians discovered a key of power in Leviticus 6:13, where the Lord says, *"Fire shall be kept burning continually on the altar; it is not to go out."* They believed the New Covenant fire on the altar was prayer, and they acted on God's challenge. The Moravians actually managed to change the world with that little key. Let me quote a brief article by Leslie K. Tarr that describes these remarkable people:

A Prayer Meeting That Lasted 100 Years[2]

Fact: The Moravian community of Herrnhut in Saxony, in 1727, commenced an around-the-clock "prayer watch" that continued non-stop for over a hundred years.

Fact: By 1792, 65 years after the commencement of that prayer vigil, the small Moravian community had sent forth 300 missionaries to the ends of the earth!

Could it be that there is some relationship between those two facts? Is fervent intercession a basic component in world evangelization? The answer to both questions is surely an unqualified "yes."

The heroic 18th century evangelization thrust of the Moravians has not received the attention it deserves. But even less heralded than their missionary exploits is that one-hundred-year prayer meeting that sustained the fires of evangelism!

During its first five years of existence, the Herrnhut settlement showed few signs of spiritual power. By the beginning of 1727, the community of about three hundred people was wracked by dissension and bickering, an unlikely site for revival.

Zinzendorf and others, however, covenanted to pray and labor for revival. On May 12, revival came. Christians were aglow with new life and power, and dissension vanished and unbelievers were converted.

Looking back to that day and the four glorious months that followed, Count Zinzendorf later recalled: "The whole place represented truly a visible habitation of God among men." A spirit of prayer was immediately evident in the fellowship and continued throughout that "golden summer of 1727," as the Moravians came to designate that period. In August 27 of that year, twenty-four men and twenty-four women covenanted to spend one hour each day in scheduled prayer. Some others also enlisted in the "hourly intercession."

"For over 100 years, the members of the Moravian church all shared in the 'hourly intercession.' At home and abroad, on land and sea, this prayer watch ascended unceasingly to the Lord," stated historian A.J. Lewis.

The Memorial Days of the Renewed Church of the Brethren, published in 1822, ninety-five years after the decision to initiate the prayer watch, quaintly describes the move in one sentence: "The thought struck some of the brethren and sisters that it might be well to set apart certain hours for the purpose of prayer, at which seasons all might be reminded of its excellency and be induced by the promises annexed to fervent, persevering prayer to pour out their hearts before the Lord."

The journal further cites Old Testament typology as warrant for the prayer watch: "*The sacred fire was never permitted to go out on the altar* (Leviticus 6:13); so in the congregation is a temple of the loving God, wherein He has His altar and fire, the intercession of His saints should incessantly rise up to Him."

That prayer watch was instituted by a community of believers whose average age was probably thirty. Zinzendorf himself was twenty-seven.

The prayer vigil by Zinzendorf and the Moravian community sensitized them to attempt the unheard-of-mission to reach others for Christ. Six months after the beginning of the prayer watch, the count suggested to his fellow Moravians the challenge of a bold evangelism aimed at the West Indies, Greenland, Turkey, and Lapland. Some were skeptical, but Zinzendorf persisted. Twenty-six Moravians stepped forward for world missions wherever the Lord led.

The exploits that followed are surely to be numbered among the high moments of Christian history. Nothing daunted Zinzendorf or his fellow heralds of Jesus Christ—prison, shipwreck, persecution, ridicule, plague, abject poverty, and threats of death. His hymn reflected his conviction:

Ambassador of Christ, know ye the way to go? It leads unto the jaws of death, is strewn with thorns and woe.

Church historians look to the eighteenth century and marvel at the Great Awakening in England and America, which swept hundreds of thousands into God's Kingdom. John Wesley figured largely in that mighty movement and much attention is centered on him. Is it not possible that we have overlooked the place which that round-the-clock prayer watch had in reaching Wesley and, through him and his associates, in altering the course of history?

One wonders what would flow from a commitment on the part of twentieth century Christians to institute a "prayer watch" for world evangelization, specifically, to reach those in Zinzendorf's words, "For whom no one cared."

In the first chapter I briefly described my encounter with the Lord along with other intercessors in the Moravian watchtower at Herrnhut. But the full story is a miraculous tale of one little key after another falling into place until God positioned us in the Spirit to receive His commission and empowerment of prayer. In fact, it was a "little key" that played one of the most prominent roles in that appointment with destiny.

After the Lord spoke to me about the restoration of the "ancient tool" of the Watch of the Lord, the study of the Watch of the Lord became one of the passions of my life. In February of 1993, I took the intercessor team mentioned in the first chapter to the Czech Republic for some intercessory prayer assignments concerning that resurrected nation, but our real mission was to cross the border to Herrnhut in ancient Saxony in East Germany to recover the anointing of the Moravian prayer watch.

KEYS OF REVELATION

As we prepared in prayer in advance of the trip, the Lord gave me several keys in the Spirit. I didn't know what they meant at the time, but I wrote them down and watched and waited. The Holy Spirit said, "You are going to find a man named Christian Winter, and he has a key." (I had never met this man or heard of him before.) The Lord also mentioned the number "37." In the days that followed, the Lord led us to Ezekiel 37 (which describes the valley of dead men's bones that God resurrected into a mighty army) and to Revelation 3:7 (where the Word speaks of "the key of David").

When we first arrived in Herrnhut, our team didn't do the usual tourist things. We didn't go to museums or famous churches, look at the sights, or go shopping. We were told to go to a certain place and meet a certain man who would direct us to our housing. We also learned that visitors were allowed to go up into the Herrnhut watchtower on occasion, but you had to have a key to enter it. As it turned out, the man we were sent to, who took us to our place of lodging, was the unofficial steward of the Moravian tower. *His name was Christian Winter!* Was this an accident? A coincidence? There's more.

Christian Winter, who has since graduated to Heaven to receive his reward, eagerly handed me the key to the Moravian watchtower when I explained our mission. But God had more in mind. I didn't know it, but this gentleman carried in his heart a divine promise that the Watch of the Lord would be restored! I felt led to deliver an expression to this stranger, someone I'd known for a matter of moments: "The Lord is restoring the ancient Watch of the Lord for which many have waited so long! You have faithfully held the key. Now the Lord will unlock the door and restore the ancient fire."

When Christian Winter looked up, he said, "You are the third man who has spoken this very same word to me."

Our prayer team spent hours in prayer in seclusion before venturing out to the Moravian prayer tower. On February 18, we walked together through the narrow streets of Herrnhut toward the cemetery the Moravians called "God's Acre." We thought that we were just going to pass through the cemetery to reach the tower, and we saw the graves of famous Moravian leaders such as Count Zinzendorf and Anna and David Nitschmann, along with those of many of the missionaries who sold themselves into slavery to take the gospel into closed nations and cultures.

As we began walking through the cemetery, there was a sobering sense that there was something—some anointing or power—that these departed saints had walked in. But this anointing seemed to be dead or long departed. I again was reminded of the Lord's word about "37," and how the Lord had led us earlier to the riveting prophecy in Ezekiel 37 concerning the valley of dead men's bones that were resurrected into a mighty army of God.

VALLEY OF DRY BONES

We felt that we needed to just sit down and wait on the Lord for some reason. We knew that the Spirit of God wanted us to pray, to deal with something in some way before we went on. So we all sat down in the middle of the cemetery and continued to wait. I know this sounds bizarre, but I happened to glance down at the grave marker by which I had made my seat and felt a thrill of the Spirit run through my body—I was sitting on the gravestone of Christian David, the man Count von Zinzendorf called "the Moravian Moses." He founded the community in 1722 and led ten different groups of refugee brethren to the lands the Count donated to the tiny Christian community. Now Christian David's tombstone was not one of the major marked tombstones. Again, was this an accident? A coincidence? Although reason could not explain these things, I could not flatly deny the possibility of coincidence at this point. I couldn't help but remember that "little keys open big doors."

As I noted earlier, I sensed that, like Ezekiel of old, we were again sitting in a valley of dry bones and that God was again asking us, "Can these bones live again?" Ezekiel identified the dry bones he saw with the broken, fragmented structures of Judaism in his day. We were sitting in that cemetery marking some of the richest prayer, devotion, and missionary endeavor in Church history. When the Lord seemed to ask us anew, "Can these bones live?," we began quietly to confess the sin of the Church. We confessed our prayerlessness through the generations, our own individual sins, and the sin of the current-day Church. And we begin to confess that the Church had dropped the baton of the spirit of prayer.

It was a quiet time of confession. There was no "travail" or weeping; there were no so-called "wild manifestations." We were just calmly confessing our sin before the Lord. After a few minutes had passed, we sensed that we "had permission" to proceed to the tower.

THE PROCESSION BEGINS

My wife, Michal Ann, seemed to take the lead at that point along with Susan Shea (now Susan Nichols), a gifted intercessor and dancer. They began to lead us up the hill with prophetic song and procession before the Lord. We weren't consciously superimposing any preconceived ideas or structure on the process; the Lord seemed to be leading us in a spiritual procession of ascents similar to what you see in the Psalms. We had come by the

Spirit with a call to restore something ancient to something new, and God was doing the work.

When we reached the tower I took out the key that Christian Winter had given me and then it hit me: I was holding the "key of David" that the Spirit had described! The key to the power and effectiveness of the Moravian community was their single-hearted devotion to Jesus Christ and to the Watch of the Lord. No one in modern Church history has wielded this "ancient tool" so effectively or faithfully as Christian David, Count von Zinzendorf, and the Moravian believers.

The "key of David" in my hand looked like a very old skeleton key, but it worked. I opened the door to the spiral staircase leading to the tower and we started climbing. As soon as we reached the top, we began to engage the Spirit through prayer. I've already described the two waves of intercession that swept over us, followed by two strong wind blasts. Yet, it is appropriate to add some details here that I purposely left out in my initial account in the first chapter.

It is difficult to exaggerate the ferocity and depth of the burden of the Lord that came over us! My wife and my sister, Barbara, were there with me, along with Sue Kellough, a prophetic intercessor from Indianapolis who is also a respected friend, advisor, and co-laborer with our ministry. Nearby stood James Nichols, a fervent African-American believer whose ancestors came from St. Thomas in the Virgin Islands where they first received the gospel from Moravian missionaries dispatched to serve the slave

The key to the power and effectiveness of the Moravian community was their single-hearted devotion to Jesus Christ and to the Watch of the Lord. No one in modern Church history has wielded this "ancient tool" so effectively or faithfully as Christian David, Count von Zinzendorf, and the Moravian believers.

population of that former Danish colony hundreds of years earlier. We were all crowded together when the first wave of intercession and groaning travail swept over us. Michal Ann remembers the scene well:

> I was just totally overcome by the Holy Spirit in that intense place of prayer. I started crying uncontrollably, and at first it seemed almost inappropriate. The whole group began to stagger under the weight of the burden, but God seemed to use me as an unwitting igniter to ignite a fire that spread through the whole group.

> The intercession that broke out was so intense that people began falling down or doubling over until they fell to the wood floor of the tower. Jim often teaches about being "possessed for prayer," and I think the Spirit of God literally began praying through us as we yielded to Him—we were all consumed with this spirit of intercession.

> The best way I know how to say it is that I felt the sorrow and the grief of the Holy Spirit. I could sense His grief and His longing for something holy and powerful to be released. I want to say it was very emotional, but I felt like I was crying from deep within my soul on behalf of the Holy Ghost. I felt like we were expressing His pain through unspeakable groanings of the Spirit. I can't bring definition to it. All I know is that I was experiencing "feelings" from His heart to my heart.

> I was so caught up in this intense place of prayer that I wasn't thinking of anything else. I don't even remember any particular Scripture coming to my mind. I was just totally focused on this burden that weighed so heavily on me. It was very deep, very concentrated, and very focused. It was a place of vulnerability, and I allowed myself to be so overcome and overwhelmed by God's Spirit that I eagerly yielded to His praying through me. It was like entering the childbirth process. When the time of birth comes, you're exposed, and you're absolutely vulnerable and naked. You

can only focus on one thing—bringing forth the baby at its appointed time.

I remember that some people responded to the weight of the spirit of travail coming on them by falling to the floor or by doubling over. We were pressed together, and it felt kind of cold in the tower at first. However, all that was forgotten once we entered this place of abandoned prayer. We were praying "as one man." It was just like a big fire that got ignited. It just overtook everybody. We were all very focused in that place.

Suddenly, the prayer burden lifted and the wind came. Some of the people from Atlanta were running a tape recorder at the time, and you can actually hear on the tape the wind roaring through the place. The wind and the travail finally died down, but it was only a "breather." The burden of the Lord came on us again. With one voice we began to travail by the Spirit as if we were instruments in the hands of our invisible God. The violent wind once again swept through the Moravian lookout prayer tower. I felt as though the wind came to blow that ancient prayer anointing throughout the world according to the spirit of grace we had just asked for.

A great joy came over us and we started marching around on the watchtower. We were rejoicing in the Lord. Then we felt the Spirit release a quickening faith in us to loose or dispatch the spirit of grace for the Watch of the Lord into different countries and cities around the world. The Lord was releasing grace for the house of prayer for all nations, and for the Watch of the Lord to be released first in 120 cities across the earth, and then to 3,000 in the pattern of the Book of Acts. God was supernaturally and symbolically fulfilling the prophecy that I'd received on the plains of Kansas two years earlier. The ancient tool of the Watch of the Lord was being released anew on the earth by the winds of God.

LEADERS OF THE PACK TODAY

There are many others who also carry this torch for unceasing prayer and the Watch of the Lord. Among them are:

1. Our friends and mentors, Mahesh and Bonnie Chavda, who have promoted all-night "Watches of the Lord" on Friday nights to build a "wall of prayer" since 1995, when the Lord showed them that corporate intercession was the missing link between renewal and the coming harvest. Join them and others in an all night prayer meeting to make history before the throne of God!

2. Lou Engle, former associate pastor at Harvest Rock Church in Pasadena, California, who has carried a burden for "24-hour houses of prayer." He has been praying for revival for decades and has launched The Call – a global prayer and fasting movement to engage in desperate actions for desperate times. (For more on this subject read our co-authored book *The Elijah Revolution*.)

3. The late Dr. Bill Bright of Campus Crusade for Christ, who in 1994 called for 2 million North Americans to fast and pray for revival for 40 days by the year 2000. This was the fruit of a 40-day fast conducted at the request of the Lord. Dr. Bright's book, *The Coming Revival*, predicts that a major worldwide revival will cover the earth by the turn of the century.

4. Wesley Campbell, founder of Revival Now! And Be a Hero Ministries in British Columbia, who has called for 100,000 intercessors to fast and pray in 40-day cycles. This modern-day revivalist warns that "our response [to the call to intercession] now is critical to the magnitude of the outpouring."[3]

5. Mike Bickle, friend, coworker, and senior leader of the International House of Prayer in Kansas City, Missouri, has prayed with his team in harp and bowl gatherings non-stop for over 8 years for an unprecedented awakening and worldwide revival.

6. C. Peter Wagner, Cindy Jacobs, Dutch Sheets, Chuck Pierce and hundreds of others intercessors, have directed global prayer initiatives for the 10/40 and 40/70 Prayer Window and have launched prayer networks across the world.

7. Tom Hess, who is the founder of the House of Prayer for All Nations on the Mount of Olives in Jerusalem, Israel, has called forth prayer watches around the clock for years.

8. Dick Simmons, who is the founder of Men for Nations in our nation's capital, has been used to release an impartation of the spirit of prayer into my life and hundreds of leaders.

On the day of Pentecost when the Holy Spirit was first given, there was the wind, fire, and wine. There was conviction and evangelization, there were signs and wonders, and there were gifts given. Best of all, there was a simple presentation of this glorious man named Christ Jesus. Now on this "second Pentecost" to the Church, we are seeing wine (in the sweet blessings and comfort of the renewal), fire (in the fiery preaching, soul winning, repentance, and call to salvation and revival by Steve Hill and others), and now the wind of the Lord signaling a great harvest. There has never been a greater need for intercession than now.

Dear God, I want to be vigilant and awake in this hour. Wake me up if you have to! I want to be a practical part of the watch of the Lord for my city. Equip me and use me as one of your Last Day Watchers. Place me in your global prayer army and send mentors my way so I can be effective in this historic move of God! Bless you Lord for including me in Your growing prayer army! Praise the Lord!

ENDNOTES

1. Strong's, **watch** (Greek #1127).

2. Leslie K. Tarr, "A Prayer Meeting."

3. Wesley Campbell, "100,000 Intercessors!" *Spread the Fire*, Vol. 2, Issue 6 (Toronto Airport Christian Fellowship, December 1996), 15.

CHAPTER 6

Restoring the Path From Prayer to His Presence

"The greatest hindrance to Christianity today is Christians who do not know how to practice the presence of God."

—Rev. Billy Graham

There should be one primary distinguishing characteristic of the people of God. It is not so much the clothes we wear, the style of our hair, or even the rules by which we conduct ourselves. But there is a "birthmark" of sorts that should set apart every community of true believers, and it should manifest itself in love for one another. Moses reveals this birthmark in a dialogue with God recorded in Exodus 33:14-16:

> *And He said, "My presence shall go with you, and I will give you rest." Then he [Moses] said to Him, "**If Your presence does not go with us**, do not lead us up from here. For how then can it be known that I have found favor in Your sight, I and Your people? **Is it not by Your going with us**, so that we, I and Your people, may be **distinguished** from all the other people who are upon the face of the earth?"* (Exodus 33:14-16)

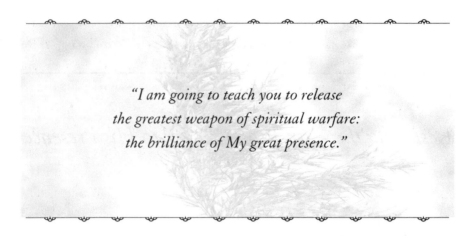

"I am going to teach you to release
the greatest weapon of spiritual warfare:
the brilliance of My great presence."

This is a key of great power in God's Kingdom. The *presence of God* is the distinguishing characteristic that proves we have favor with God! Without it, we are as other men. The glory of God is "the manifested presence of God," the visible evidence that the person of God, Himself, has shown up among us—and that is the greatest thing in life! I believe Moses was crying out to the Lord of Hosts, "Oh, Great One, do not take us up from here unless You go before us. Put *the brilliance of Your great presence* upon us."

It is no accident that one of the names and titles given Jesus Christ was Immanuel ("God with us"). This chapter was inspired by a word that the Lord planted in me while I was attending a renewal service with Michal Ann in October 1994, at what was then Toronto Airport Christian Fellowship. After we were prayed for, we remained still and quiet and waited for the Lord to speak to our hearts. The Holy Spirit began to speak to me, and He said, "I am going to teach you to release the highest weapon of spiritual warfare."

Now that made my spiritual antennas go out! I didn't say anything, but let me tell you I was ready to receive whatever God had for me. At first, the Lord simply told me, "I am going to teach you to release the greatest weapon of spiritual warfare." But finally He added, "*I will teach you to release the brilliance of My great presence*."

Not long ago, I was ministering on the East Coast of the United States when the Spirit of God dropped a sentence into my heart. He said, "I am going to reveal My raw power." I think the Church has gotten too accustomed to "refined sugar." God wants to give us something that's a little more raw and less predictable. C.S. Lewis, in his delightful series of children's books called *The Chronicles of Narnia*, repeatedly warns the central characters that "Aslan the Lion [the Christ figure] is not a *tame lion*." The Church needs to rediscover the truth that the Lion of Judah is *not a tame lion*. God is not *tame*. He cannot be controlled, limited, manipulated, or made "predictable" by mere men who believe they understand everything about God. He is God Almighty, the eternal I AM, the Alpha and Omega, the Ancient of Days. He wants to give us something that is concentrated, condensed, and volatile. He likes to jar us with a "holy jolt" from time to time just to shake us, wake us, and stir us up (but He always does it for our own good).

As I write these words, I am not where I once was, nor am I where I am going to be in the days to come. I'm in yet another season of learning. That is why I want to put a parenthesis around the statement: "I will teach you [because you aren't there yet] to release the brilliance of My great presence."

BEING A SPIRITUAL ARCHAEOLOGIST

Sometimes I feel like God has given me a pick and shovel, and a hammer and a brush—then commissioned me as a Holy Ghost archaeologist to search through the ruins of the past for His lost treasures (but I'm not complaining). There is a treasure, a jewel of the Church, that is bright and shining. It is the jewel of God's glory, the manifestation of His glorious Person in our midst. It is His incomparable presence in all its brilliance. We need to rediscover, recover, and redisplay the family Jewel! I believe God is also saying this to His Church worldwide: "I will teach you to release the brilliance of My great presence."

I often wear a cross that was given to me as a gift, and it has become very special to me. It is a Moravian cross bearing the symbol of a lamb with a flag of victory. The motto of the Moravians in the 1700s was, "To win for the Lamb the rewards for His suffering." As I noted earlier, they launched the "Watch of the Lord," a continuous prayer vigil that lasted more than a century after the Lord illuminated Count von Zinzendorf's understanding of Leviticus 6:13, which says, *"Fire shall be kept burning continually on the altar; it is not to go out."*

The Moravians, under the leadership of Count von Zinzendorf, recognized the power in the key of the Lord revealed in Leviticus 6. So they decided to accept the task of keeping a continual fire of prayer, intercession, and worship burning before the Lord's presence. I doubt if they realized they would actually keep the fire burning hot and pure for more than 100 years, but they began by making personal commitments to the task.

At first, a total of 48 women and 48 men signed up to pray. Two men prayed together and two women prayed together for a one-hour watch until the next team relieved them. This pattern continued around the clock, day after day and week after week, for more than 100 years! The fervent heat generated by the sacrificial fire of their sustained prayer ignited revival fires that launched their pioneering missionary efforts and helped birth the first great awakening through their godly influence on men such as John and Charles Wesley.

All this ties in with the simple revelation that God gave me in the Czech Republic. What I've already mentioned bears repeating again. God asked me, "Have you ever considered the multidirectional dimension of prayer?" Then, He said, *"Remember, what goes up must come down."*

Our prayers ascend to God as sweet-smelling *incense*, and He responds by sending them back down to earth as answered prayers accompanied by His fire. The Old Testament describes in detail the special incense offered to God in the tabernacle of Moses each day:

> *And you shall put this altar in front of the veil that is near the ark of the testimony, in front of the mercy seat that is over the ark of the testimony,* **where I will meet with you.** *And Aaron shall burn* **fragrant incense** *on it; he shall burn it every morning when he trims the lamps. And when Aaron trims the lamps at twilight, he shall burn incense. There shall be* **perpetual incense** *before the Lord throughout your generations* (Exodus 30:6-8).

> *Then the Lord said to Moses, "Take for yourself spices, stacte and onycha and galbanum, spices with pure frankincense; there shall be an equal part of each. And with it you shall make incense, a perfume, the work of*

a perfumer, salted, pure, and holy. And you shall beat some of it very fine, and put part of it before the testimony in the tent of meeting, where I shall meet with you; it shall be most holy to you" (Exodus 30:34-36).

In the New Testament, we are commanded to "pray without ceasing" (1 Thess. 5:17). This perfectly parallels God's command to Moses and Aaron concerning the sweet odor of "perpetual incense" that was to continually waft into the Most Holy Place from the altar of incense. When I first began to study these verses in the Book of Exodus, my mind went into gear and I thought: *Now it's logical that if I can get an understanding of what each one of these ingredients is, then perhaps it will give me some insight into what God receives as an acceptable sacrifice of prayer.*

WHAT ARE THE INGREDIENTS OF PRAYER?

It is extremely interesting that God says these four ingredients must be mixed in equal proportions. That is a reference to balance. A lot of people (including me) have taught technical procedural steps of prayer labeled with titles like, "The Seven Steps to Answered Prayer." These sermons are good and mostly valid in content, but there really aren't seven steps to answered prayer. The reality that I've discovered is that prayer isn't a technique. It isn't a thing at all. Neither is prayer a methodology. Prayer is communion with a Person. Prayer is simply *being with God.*

Despite all of the elaborate rituals and steps of purification laid down in the Law of Moses, David, the shepherd-king, bypassed it all to sit in the shadow of the ark of the covenant on Mount Zion and commune heart to heart with God

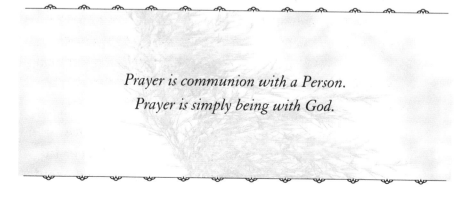

Prayer is communion with a Person.
Prayer is simply being with God.

(see 1 Chron. 17:16). He didn't have the bloodlines or credentials of an Aaronic priest, nor did he belong to the tribe of Levi. Although only the high priest was allowed in the Most Holy Place, and then only on one day of the year, David literally sat before the Lord, perhaps on many occasions. Why? Because prayer is communion, and David had a heart after God's own heart. (This is even more amazing when you realize that all of this happened *before* Jesus died on the Cross and removed the veil between God and man. The intensity of David's love overcame the barrier between him and his God.)

We have to push past even the correct technical methodologies to get to the heart of God Himself. We must get Him. We must have Him. I know the Old Testament talks about coming into God's courts with praise and His gates with thanksgiving, but the issue is not the technique. The issue is a Person. We're coming to our Father. We're coming to His glorious Son who loves us, who knows us, who gave His life for us. We're coming before the One whom the Book of John says *"is in the bosom of the Father"* (John 1:18).

More Than a Methodology

I even feel a little hesitant to talk about the four qualities of the incense of prayer, but if we can avoid turning it into a methodology, it will help us in our journey from prayer into His brilliant presence.

1. **Stacte** was a sweet spice. It was found on or near the northern border of Israel and in Syria. It took a full day's journey by foot to reach the trees that oozed forth the resin that was baked until the spice, called *stacte*, emerged. Both the Greek and Hebrew names for this spice mean "to ooze forth or to drop." It was used at times as a metaphor for the emergence of the Word of God or for the act of prophesying. In both cases, it creates the picture of something that has been stored up inside of you oozing or bubbling out from an inner abundance.

   When we store up the *logos*, or written Word of God, within our hearts then, when the wind of God breathes upon it, it may become a spoken, revelatory *rhema* Word into our lives. The first quality of acceptable incense of prayer is a rich store of the Word of God in our lives, which oozes forth upon demand to drop onto other people. Prayer is abiding in the living Word, which is obviously Christ.

It will cost you something to store the Word of God in your life. It will cost you time and a priority shift. It generally will land you in difficult circumstances, but it is worth it. Once you fill your heart with this sweet spice of God's Word, it will ooze forth from every pore of your life and being and permeate your prayers with a sweetness that pleases God and blesses everyone it touches.

2. **Onycha** refers to finely ground aromatic powder produced from a mollusk shell found in the Mediterranean Sea. Although the distance involved to get onycha was less than that for stacte, this powder could be obtained only by making a lengthy trip to the sea to gather a particular type of mollusk or mussel. The mollusk shells were ground into a fine powder and then burned with fire to produce the sweet fragrance so vital to the holy incense.

   Our lives should continually release an aroma of fragrant offering unto the Lord. But how does onycha from the Old Testament incense mixture fit into this picture? Have you ever felt like you have been "ground into a pulp" or been broken into little pieces by a trial or circumstance? Have you been "burned" by the thoughtless or deliberate actions of other people? The prayer you offer after enduring these events bears the fragrance of onycha. Scarred prayer warriors reek of onycha. Prayer is a lifestyle of brokenness before God; prayer is communion bathed in the sweet fragrance of a crushed spice called humility and brokenness. David wrote from the depths of brokenness, *"The sacrifices of God are a broken spirit; a broken and a contrite heart, O God, You will not despise"* (Ps. 51:17).

3. **Galbanum** is "a yellowish to green or brown aromatic bitter gum resin derived from several Asian plants."[1] The original Hebrew word, *chelbenah*, meaning "richness or fatness," implies that galbanum comes from the richest or choice part.[2] Galbanum is the oily substance that is used to *hold all the other elements together*.

The overriding conviction that "God is good" will hold your life together and help bring unity among brethren who have different qualities and varying beliefs. Too often we have allowed ourselves to divide into "camps" based on particular areas of truth or emphasis. For example, people of the "Word camp" eat the Word of God. They know the Word, they love the Word, they preach the Word, they proclaim the Word, and they pray the Word—sometimes at the expense of mercy and brokenness. The "brokenness camp" includes many "revival-type people," who at times seem to be in an unspoken competition to see who can get the lowest so God can be the highest. That's all well and good, but it is only one piece of a greater whole. We need all the camps and their corresponding truths working together. We need an equal proportion of the extravagance, richness, and fatness of our good God to bind us all together in harmony.

My wife, Michal Ann, recently received an amazing God Encounter. The manifested presence came into our bedroom and a voice spoke to her and said, "Receive the goodness of God into your body." Since then she has done a word study on "goodness and mercy". Believe me, you will be hearing more about this in the future. This has rocked her world and sending her into another orbit. Receive the goodness of God right now into your life! It will transform you!

To receive anything from God, you *must believe that He is, and that He is a rewarder of those who seek Him*" (Heb. 11:6b). We must believe that He who freely gave His Son will also freely give us all things. We must believe in the richness, the fatness and the goodness of God.

4. **Frankincense** is "a resin [obtained] from the bark of trees of the genus Boswellia. As the amber resin dries, white dust forms on the drops or tears of frankincense, thus giving rise to its Semitic name. In biblical times most frankincense came either from or via Sheba in southern Arabia."[3] The Hebrew word for frankincense is

> *Only freshly made incense would do.*
> *You and I can't live on the prayers*
> *of the past. We can't thrive on*
> *the relationship, the intimacy,*
> *or the communion that we*
> *enjoyed with the Lord yesterday.*

lavona, which literally means "to be white."[4] Perhaps this fore-shadowed the righteousness we received when Christ, the scion or branch of David, hung on a tree and shed His blood. By the time the blood of the Lamb dried on the tree and the earth, we were made "the righteousness of God in Christ" by God's grace and love. It is the blood, shed and applied to us, that cleanses us from all sin. It is through the blood that we are dressed in white and made fit for the Kingdom.

FRESHLY MADE

It is important to remember that the ingredients for the holy incense were purchased fresh each day and mixed in equal proportions. The incense could not be "stored up." Only freshly made incense would do. You and I can't live on the prayers of the past. We can't thrive on the relationship, the intimacy, or the communion that we enjoyed with the Lord *yesterday*.

Day by day, we must make our way into His presence to be renewed, transformed, empowered, and filled with His glory. We have been commissioned to light the fire of prayer and offer sweet-smelling incense created from equal parts of *stacte*, the oozing, bubbling abundance of God's indwelling Word; *onycha*, the sweet crushed spice of inward humility and brokenness; *galbanum*, the unyielding and ingathering faith that God is good; and the purity *of frankincense*, the righteousness of Christ applied and dried upon our hearts in whiteness and holiness unto the Lord.

The priests of old tended the fire of God and carried sweet incense and fire into the Holy of Holies. The priests wore white linen garments adorned with alternating bells and pomegranates on the hem. This speaks of the double blessing of God. The Lord revealed to me as I prayed for my wife that He longs to anoint us with a double blessing, just as Elisha received when Elijah ascended to Heaven. God gave the Church nine gifts (signified by the bells signaling that the priests of God are alive and well), and nine fruit of the Spirit (signified by the pomegranates). When we enter His presence, we are going for the "double blessing" of the fullness of God's character and the fullness of His power.

It was in God's presence—beyond the veil of separation—that the priests of Aaron approached the ark of the covenant containing symbols of the authority of God (signified by Aaron's rod that budded); the provision of God in the bread of life (marked by a pot of the manna God sent from Heaven); the rule and order of God (symbolized by the stone tablets containing the Ten Commandments). All of these could only be approached through mercy, symbolized by the seat of mercy situated between the covering cherubs of God.

This is a beautiful picture of the genuine Church of the redeemed, a Church filled with the sweet-smelling smoke of prayer, praise, worship, and intercession. It is here in the presence that God says, "I will commune with you there." It is here that we see an abundance of holy gifts, fruit, incense, holiness, mercy, authority, and the sovereign rule of God in the bounds of covenant love.

The secret to maturity and purity in the Church is found in the path from prayer to His presence. We *must* get the distinguishing characteristic of the genuine people of God! There was no *natural light* in the Most Holy Place because it wasn't needed or welcome. Just as the Scriptures tell us that God Himself shall be the light to His people, in His presence we need no natural light (natural or earthbound knowledge or man's wisdom). The only light bathing the Most Holy Place is the light of His brilliant, shining presence. In our day, we call this light the *shekinah* glory—the manifested glory or presence of God.

A Dilemma Resolved

Prayer, particularly intercessory prayer, has played a key role in my life and ministry for years. I like a fight. I love to see the works of the devil destroyed. So I have been pondering the various doctrines concerning spiritual warfare, and I've examined my personal experiences in the light of God's Word. I've met with different intercessory leaders around the world to increase my understanding on the controversial issues dealing with principalities, powers, and other things of this nature. God just solved the whole thing for me when He told me, "I'm going to teach you the highest weapon of spiritual warfare—it is releasing the brilliance of My great presence." Do you want to win? Get soaked in His presence!

When you get around somebody who smokes, the odor of the smoke permeates your clothing (and lungs) so effectively that other people will think you smoke, too! Why? Because the odor of the smoke gets all over you. When you start spending time with God, the *same thing* happens. In the realm of men, people won't be able to describe it, perhaps, but they will be drawn to the fragrance of mercy, grace, and life that will permeate your being. In the spirit realm, the demons of hell will start thinking that you look a little bit like God—you smell like Him; you glow with a deadly light that they fear. Your presence will remind them of His presence. The smoke that surrounds the mercy seat of God will be absorbed by your spirit. The atmosphere of Heaven will get into you.

Issues of the Heart

How do you go from prayer to His presence? It's a heart issue. I'm not going to give you five steps. I can't because I don't know them (although I used to think that I did). All I can tell is something like Heidi Baker in Mozambique, Africa, "God is looking for laid down lovers!" So let's just lay down our lives and learn mercy, and God will meet you to commune with you there.

Hebrews 4:16 tells us, *"Let us therefore draw near with confidence to the throne of grace, that we might receive mercy and may find grace to help in time of need."* Jesus said, *"But go and learn what this means. I desire compassion* [mercy KJV] *and not sacrifice, for I did not come to call the righteous, but sinners"* (Matt. 9:13). God communes with us at the seat of mercy. It doesn't go away; it is the very atmosphere and environment of God's presence.

This gets to the core of what we call religion. Man's religion is judgment pending criticism, legalism, and debate. God does not want us operating out of judgment. He wants us operating out of the seat of mercy.

A man named Rex Andrews walked with the Lord but fell away in the 1940s. Then God reached out in His mercy and changed him, and he returned to the Lord. The presence of God was restored to him in a moment. In 1944, at the height of World War II, God gave this man a revelation through a gift of prophecy of what mercy is. God told him:

Mercy is God's supply system for every need everywhere. Mercy is that kindness, compassion, and tenderness, which is a passion to suffer with or participate in another's ills or evils in order to relieve, heal, and restore—to accept another freely and gladly as he is—and to supply the need of the good of life to build up, to bring to peace, and keep in peace. It is to take another into one's heart just as he is, to cherish and nourish him there. Mercy takes another's sins, evils, and faults as its own and frees the other by bearing them to God. This is called the glow of love. This is the anointing.

I'm not who I was. I'm not who I yet want to be.
I long to be a person of His presence—one who
spends time with Him and then releases the brilliance
of His great presence to the world around me.

Even though we store up the Word, ask for the cross of brokenness, walk in the reality that God is good and that we are bound together by His extravagance, His richness, and His fatness, and clothe ourselves in the gift of righteousness made available to us through the blood of Jesus—there is something more. When we take this freshly mixed incense, offer it on the fires of fervent prayer, and take it beyond the veil, *there is still one more necessary thing*. We need to have *mercy* built into our lives.

I long to be a person of His presence. I'm not who I was. I'm not who I yet want to be. I long to be a person of His presence—one who spends time with Him and then releases the brilliance of His great presence to the world around me. The Lord is looking for such a people who will simply come and *be with Him*. He wants a nation of kings and priests who diligently will go from prayer to His presence and bear the distinguishing characteristic of His people—*God with us*.

I believe that the Church has been corporately ministering at the altar of incense for the last 20 years, but, in one sense, has never gone inside where His presence abides. Now, it is as though we are crossing over the threshold and through the veil into the place of His manifested presence. It is a new beginning, a fresh start. That's why there's a new wind blowing across the earth, a wind called renewal, revival—and a hunger for a great awakening to come.

What is the Lord requiring of us? He is calling us to be with Him. It's time to cross over, to abide in His presence: "Come, come, come!" says the Lord. "Come, come, come before Me."

Prayer is not a technique. Prayer is not a methodology. Prayer is not a matter of "steps one, two, and three." It is our coming to a Person and being saturated with the communion of His great and glorious presence. God is restoring the fire on the altar in His Church today. During the last 15 to 20 years, renewed fires of prayer have circled the earth. That is marvelous! It is the first time that these renewed fires have burst forth to this degree on a global scale. But, I want to tell you that God is at the brink of taking us even deeper—because this is not a matter of technique or know-how. It doesn't hinge on what seminars we go to or whose tape sets or DVDs we buy. The Church is learning anew what the Moravians and others discovered almost half a millennium ago. The greatest thing in life is to be able to touch the heart of God and have His heart touch you. It is time to enter and bask in His brilliant presence.

Teach me to release the highest weapon of spiritual warfare – the brilliance of your great presence. I want to be a contagious carrier of your infectious presence. Like Moses I cry, "Let Your presence go before me!" I choose to spend time with You Lord, so that I will be armed with Your might, power and presence. For Your honor and glory sake! Amen!

ENDNOTES

1. *Merriam-Webster's Collegiate Dictionary, 10*th *Edition,* All.

2. Strong's, **galbanum** (#2464).

3. R. Laird Harris, Gleason L. Archer, Jr., Bruce K. Waltke, eds. *Theological Wordbook of the Old Testament,* Vol. 1 (Chicago, IL: Moody Press, 1980), lebona, **frankincense** (#1074.4), 468.

4. Strong's, **frankincense** (#3828).

CHAPTER 7

Restoring the House of Prayer for All Nations

Jesus said, "Is it not written, 'My house shall be called a house of prayer for all the nations'?" (see Mark 11:17)

I am grateful to be alive today. We're seeing the Son of God enter His Father's house again with fiery zeal to turn the tables on the agendas of wayward men. Once again the Lamb of God has stormed into His Papa's house with the zeal of the Lord of Hosts eating Him up. He isn't content just to turn over our tables of religious pomp and circumstance and man-pleasing programs. He is moving on to the cages that we've constructed with our rigid religion to confine and control the Dove of God, the Holy Spirit! I can almost hear Him say, "My Dove, men have thought to keep You in a cage, but I am going to rattle this cage once again and send You forth. For where the Spirit of the Lord is, there is liberty."

I can almost imagine the scene in the temple of Herod, when a commotion arose on one side as the Spirit of God moved upon the children in the temple. I can imagine the Spirit causing even the smallest little children to prophesy and sing praises in ecstasy. Almost out loud, I can hear the disapproving murmurs of the religious crowd, "It hasn't been seen this way before, and we don't like it."

The zeal of the Lord of Hosts is loose in the land. The power and anointing in the Church is escalating as God releases the zeal of the Father's house upon His people. It brings holy boldness and an unquenchable spirit of prayer. It stems from the holy jealousy of God who is declaring in a loud voice, "I'm coming to take over My house and to claim My house for My own." In the Spirit, I can hear Jesus declare to this generation of believers:

"You have made My house into a den of thieves, but I say that My Father's house shall be called **a house of prayer for all the nations**. As it was in the last days of My earthly ministry, so shall it be in the last days of My ministry in the earth by the power of the Holy Spirit. Zeal for My Father's house will come upon you, and there will be a declaration that shall go forth in the latter days.

There will be an understanding that will go forth: The Father's house is not first the house of preaching. The Father's house is not first the house of sacraments. The Father's house is not first a house of fellowship or supernatural gifts. My Father's house shall have many of these things, but My Father's house shall be known first as a house of prayer for all nations—of people being built together, holy, on fire, compassionate; of living stones being brought together as they seek My face. And there will be a smoke that shall come forth from these living stones being built together. And the smoke signal shall rise up to the highest heaven and will be received. This smoke is called the incense of prayer."
(See Psalm 69:9 and John 2:17.)

In Mark 11:17, Jesus said, "...*Is it not written, 'My* **house shall be called a house of prayer for all the nations'**? *But you have made it a* **robbers' den.**" Jesus Christ personally cleansed the temple of merchandisers who had desecrated and defiled His Father's "house of prayer." All four Gospels carefully record this demonstration of the jealousy of God (see Matt. 21:12-13; Mark 11:15-17; Luke 19:45; John 2:14). John's account says that Jesus personally fashioned a whip with cords for the task. The Lord condemned the actions of men by saying in effect, "You changed My Father's house and made it into something that it should never become! You have made it into a den of thievery." Christ quoted from the scroll of Isaiah before He declared that the will, the purpose, and the heart of the Father had been violated (see Isa. 56:7).

He said the house of God was to be marked for prayer for all nations. The Greek word for nations is *ethnos*. God intended for His "house of prayer" to take a worldwide "redemptive intercessory posture" that extends far beyond Israel. Every believer in this royal priesthood is called to worship, praise, prayer, and intercession.

Although prayer or worship is never specifically listed among the spiritual grace gifts, *charisma* in the Greek, like the gift of faith or the gift of discerning of spirits, we do find an anointing upon the Levitical priesthood of the Old Testament that foreshadows the anointing on the new order of priests under the blood. Instead of one small family being set aside to be worshipers, God marked an entire nation of faith with blood as His own.

WHERE IS PRAYER ON THE GIFT LIST?

Ephesians chapter 4 describes the leadership gifts (*doma* in the Greek) of apostles, prophets, evangelists, pastors, and teachers, but prayer and worship specifically are not listed there. Yet after quizzing our Father many times, I have come to the strong conviction that God purposefully omitted them. Why? Because as New Testament believers before God the Father and His Christ, we are each called before the throne of God to offer continual sacrifices of worship, praise, and prayer (including intercession).

Worship is the act and attitude of wholeheartedly giving yourself to God with all of your spirit, soul, and body. The Greek word translated as "worship" is *proskuneo*. It means "to kiss, like a dog licking his master's hand; to prostrate oneself in homage, reverence, and adoration" (see Matt. 4:10). Jesus told the Samaritan woman at the well that God was looking for those who would worship Him in spirit and in truth (see John 4:23).[1]

Intercession means to make a request to a superior. Prayer is our means of asking our loving Father God for His intervention on our behalf night and day (see Luke 11:13). Prayer is our key to release His blessings to one another for salvation, healing, anointing, and every other personal and corporate need. We are supposed to offer prayers on behalf of people, cities, churches, nations, family groups, and the thousands of tribes in the earth. According to Revelation chapters 5 and 8, worship and prayer are to come together as a seamless garment worn by the priests of God—joined, united, and wed together. God is seeking people who will worship *and* pray! He told Ezekiel that He had found no one who would stand in the gap and intercede, and He was appalled (see Ezekiel 22:30).

A Heart Bowed Down

Expressions of prayer and worship continually appear together throughout the New Testament. Nearly everyone who asked Jesus to intervene in their lives or meet a need came and bowed down before Him *first*. Worship involves bowing our hearts (and bodies, at times) before God. God is looking for a people who will prostrate themselves in their heart and lavishly give themselves to praise. They will create an atmosphere for a throne of praise in which God Himself is pleased to dwell! When we prostrate ourselves and lavishly give our hearts in praise and in adoration to Him, we are creating a place in the spirit from which He will rule and reign over His enemies.

The Syro-Phoenician woman in Matthew 15:25 prostrated herself before Jesus first. Then she asked Him for a miracle. Prayer and worship are mentioned as interactive integral parts of the first church. Acts 16:25 describes how Paul and Silas, their backs stinging and bleeding, boldly prayed and worshiped God aloud—even while bound in stocks.

It was also impossible to separate praise and prayer in the Old Testament. Jewish worshipers often sang God's praise and slipped smoothly into prayer and back again. The two were uniquely interjoined and were never intended to be separated. Due to the influence of IHOP in Kansas City and other locations around the globe, the applications and terminology of the Harp and

Bowl is rather common place today. Worship and prayer is merging together as a seemless garment for the New Testament priesthood of all believers.

The Lord declared, *"Even those I will bring to My holy mountain, and make them joyful in My house of prayer"* (Isa. 56:7a). The Hebrew word for prayer

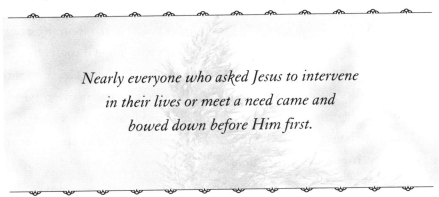

Nearly everyone who asked Jesus to intervene in their lives or meet a need came and bowed down before Him first.

here is *tephillah*. It is used to describe prayer 77 times in the Old Testament, and it refers to "intercession, supplication; by implication a *hymn*—prayer."[2] Another source implies several meanings including intercession, to the act of intervening, judgment, and broken supplication.[3]

My condensed definition of this kind of prayer is based on David the psalmist's decision to label his psalm-hymns as prayers. I call the *tephillah* the *"sung intercessory judgments of God."* This term specifically is used to title the five greatest psalms of David—Psalms 17; 86; 90; 102; and 142. It also is used in the title for the prayer of Habakkuk in Habakkuk 3:1. This was a joining together of the high priestly ministry of prayer and of praise.

In Psalm 72:20, the Bible says, *"The **prayers** of David the son of Jesse are ended."* Again, David the psalmist uses the plural of the word here, *tephillah*, meaning *"the sung intercessory judgments of God."* This reference to Psalms 1 through 72 clearly tells us that they were all "sung prayers." They were most likely set to music and sung in formal worship.

A DIVINE APPOINTMENT

Now that we better understand what the Lord means when He says His house is to be a "house of prayer for all nations," we need to go back to the number "37." After our encounter with the Lord in the watchtower at Herrnhut in 1993, Michal Ann and I took the team of intercessors to the city of Liberec in the Czech Republic. Three years earlier, in 1990, I had visited Prague with my dear brother, Mahesh Chavda, about six months after communism fell. He conducted a massive gathering where 10,000 people came, and we prayed for people for healing until 2:00 in the morning every night. One year later, I was invited to speak at their national conference in Prague, and upon its completion took my team to northern Czech to this quaint city called Liberec. One day, when the other people in our ministry team took a day off and went out touring, I stayed in my room to seek the Lord. Only one thing came to me that day. God wanted me to meet a man who had received a heavenly vision.

I was scheduled to speak at a church in the city that night, and I'd never met the leadership of the church. I didn't even know what kind of church it was. I noticed that the senior pastor wasn't on the platform, but I didn't realize that he was sitting in the congregation to the side of the platform that night. I stood up to speak, and about halfway through, the Lord had me point to this person on the side and say: "Sir, you've had a heavenly visitation. You have been taken up in the Spirit before God, and He spoke to you about ten things that are going to happen. And you are going to be used to help restore the Watch of the Lord."

I did not know that this man, Pastor Evald Rucky, was a Moravian pastor of this congregation of 13 people, which since has grown to a vibrant church of a few hundred. During communism, it had been a little group. Earlier in the year, Evald had traveled to Sweden. While he was preaching, he had a heart attack and went into a coma for a few days. His associate pastor, Peter, was also his best friend. Evald told me later that he "went on a little trip for three days" and saw the Lord. He looked down upon the globe much like Ezekiel was *"hung between Heaven and earth"* (Ezek. 8:3). Evald saw dark clouds over central Europe penetrated by white lights going up and down from the heavens. The Holy Spirit explained, "These are My angels being released in answer to the prayers of the saints." They were breaking up the black clouds, which were territorial spirits massed over central Europe.

On the third day of Evald's heavenly visit, his best friend, Peter, joined Evald's wife at the bedside of his dear friend whom he believed was sinking into an irreversible coma. Peter didn't know how to pray for his friend. Evald, whose spirit seemed to be in Heaven at the time, did not realize that he was a husband, a father, and a pastor whose work was incomplete. He was just enjoying Heaven. Then Peter began to pray a "prayer of tears" from his heart. As Peter's tears fell from his eyes and landed on Evald's body in the hospital bed, Evald suddenly began to be aware in Heaven that he was a husband, a father, and a pastor, and that his work was not yet complete. He also knew that he had a decision to make.

Within moments, Evald found himself soaring through the heavens. Then his spirit hit his body in the hospital bed. He was miraculously healed in a moment. The doctors declared it a miracle. He was released from the hospital and didn't have to pay a dime of the medical expenses! Today, I know the story well. But that night in 1991, I just said, "There's a man over here who's had a heavenly visitation." Evald responded, and the rest is history. The people in that service passed around a sign-up list. People signed

Evald [Rucky] saw dark clouds over central Europe penetrated by white lights going up and down from the heavens. The Holy Spirit explained, "These are My angels being released in answer to the prayers of the saints."

up that very night to launch a renewed Watch of the Lord—and they haven't stopped. They have one of the most vital churches in all of the Czech Republic today, and recently started several other satellite churches. I believe Evald is operating in an authentic apostolic for his nation and his denomination.

KNEELING IN THE STREETS!

So in 1993, fresh from our Herrnhut encounter, we found ourselves back in Evald's city of Liberec. We divided our prayer group into smaller teams to stay in the homes of the people there, and my wife and I led a small group to an area called Heineson where a satellite church was being planted. Michal Ann and I were walking down a little cobblestone street in the company of some of the church leaders and members when I noticed some little white objects scattered on the street.

I looked closer at these objects and felt faith start to rise up in me. I pointed them out to Michal Ann, who began to get excited, too. The objects looked like white marbles. For some reason I felt like we were supposed to pick them up. (I love the Holy Ghost. He is not only good, but He is also lots of fun.) So Michal Ann and I got down on our hands and knees to pick up these marbles on a cobblestone street in the Czech Republic while rain drizzled upon us. I think the local church leaders who were watching us were wondering if we'd lost our marbles! The truth is that we found them that day. These marbles looked like they were handmade from white stone of some kind. After we picked up every single marble, we felt led to count them while the leaders waited for us. Guess how many we found? Thirty-seven!

Little keys open big doors. The symbolic interpretation of this little incident came instantly: "The Church 'lost her marbles' some time ago, and we have lost the mind of Christ about the heavenly perspective of the eternal value of prayer!" God has something on His mind—Ezekiel 37. God is out to return His marbles, the mind of Christ, to His Church, because she's lost her way. We are regaining His eternal perspective on the value of the prayers of two or three who come together in the name of Jesus! He wants to give us back the key of power that is released when believers harmonize together in the name of Jesus.

In your life and ministry, understanding may only require one simple and humble step: Ask. My wife and I couldn't figure out why we were so excited that day in Heineson, and those local church leaders couldn't either—until we started counting our marbles. (I still have these precious 37 marbles to this day on display on our fireplace mantel.)

PRAYER PRECEDES MISSIONS

Organized missionary work and world evangelization as we know it today really didn't exist in the Western world until God lit a fire in the hearts of the Moravians through the watch of the Lord. It was no accident that God restored the fire on the altar of prayer *first*, and then He ignited a passion for lost souls in and through prayer. Let me quote from Leslie K. Tarr's account once more:

> Six months after the beginning of the prayer watch, the count [von Zinzendorf] suggested to his fellow Moravians the challenge of a bold evangelism aimed at the West Indies, Greenland, Turkey, and Lapland. Some were skeptical, but Zinzendorf persisted. Twenty-six Moravians stepped forward for world missions wherever the Lord led.[4]

By 1832, 100 years after the first missionaries left for foreign soil, 42 Moravian mission stations existed around the world. Today, membership in the Moravian mission churches outnumber those at home 4-to-1.[5]

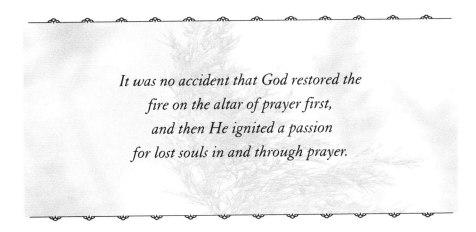

*It was no accident that God restored the
fire on the altar of prayer first,
and then He ignited a passion
for lost souls in and through prayer.*

Today, every 60 minutes about 7,000 people die, of which 6,000, do not know the Lord Jesus Christ. There are 235 geographical entities, called nations, of which 97 have been virtually closed to conventional residential missionary activity. An estimated 2.6 billion unreached people live in these closed nations in what has been called "The 10/40 and the 40/70 Window." Millions of Christians recently have banded together to pray and intercede for these people, but this one-time or two-time effort is only the beginning of what God is doing in His Church.[6]

We can see a picture of God's goal in Revelation 5:8-10. Jesus taught us to pray, *"Your will be done, on earth as it is in Heaven"* (Matt. 6:10). According to this passage in the Book of Revelation, the redeemed of God in Heaven come from every tribe, every tongue and people and nation. They were involved in unceasing worship and praise of the Lord!

HEAVEN ON EARTH

I'll never forget the wonderful sound of worship in a service held in Willemstad, the capital of the island nation of Curaso (Curacao), one of the Netherlands Antilles islands just off the coast of Venezuela where approximately 136,000 people live. What struck me was how these people worshiped! Their worship service was conducted in four languages at once! They sang in Dutch, English, Spanish, and in their own island dialect called Papiamento. It was wonderful. It was a taste of Heaven. At one moment they would sing the praises of Jesus in English; then they would sing in Dutch. They would sing "I Exalt Thee" in Spanish, then in Papiamento, and finally in English. They displayed multiple expressions in dance and in prayer. I thought, *Lord, I like this.* I felt as if He replied, "If you like *this*, wait till you get up here with Me!"

Jesus Christ is transforming us into a "house of prayer." He longs for us to lavishly pour our fears, our love, our affection, our adoration, and our tears upon His feet. He longs to hear us say again and again, "God, I lay my life before You." As we do this, He will shine His face upon us in all of His glory and say, "Go. Your feet are shod with the preparation of the gospel of peace."

In Psalm 2:8, God says, *"Ask of Me, and I will surely give the nations as Your inheritance, and the very ends of the earth as Your possession."* A lot of voices in the church world will say, "You can have the world—I don't want it. This country is going to hell—but I'm going to Heaven." Sometimes, we are too ready to give away the very thing God wants to give to us just because there are some giants in the land. God still needs some Joshuas and Calebs today.

He is looking for a people who will stand in the gap and say, "Yes, Lord, I am looking for the rewards of Christ's suffering. I'm asking for the nations as a footstool for Your marvelous feet." God wants to see a whole nation of kings and priests offer this prayer to Him with faith, power, and passion.

KEYS TO THE HARVEST

No harvest can take place without prayer for four very important reasons:

1. Only a small part of God's people are involved in seed sowing.
2. Only a small part of the seed sown actually germinates.
3. Only a small part of the seed that germinates continues growing to full harvest.
4. Only a small part of the actual harvest is fully utilized.

Your prayers can make a vital difference, especially when you harmonize in prayer with others and carefully target your prayers. Since prayer is unhindered by time, distance, or language barriers, you can join any ministry team on the earth! Teams can go constantly to sow the seed of the gospel in the earth. For God's sake, get on somebody's team. Pray for ministry leaders and help them see something make it to harvest! Remember, through prayer you can join any team! You are not confined by time, distance, or space. Ask God to guide you to the ministry or persons He wants you to support in prayer. He will burden your heart. You will become a modern-day Aaron or Hur lifting up the weary hands of your God-appointed Moses.

Your prayers can "water" the harvest and energize the seed that has been sown. Perhaps the greatest need between seedtime and harvest is rain.

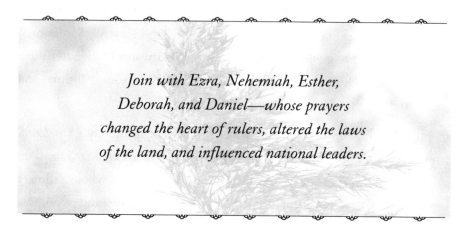

Join with Ezra, Nehemiah, Esther, Deborah, and Daniel—whose prayers changed the heart of rulers, altered the laws of the land, and influenced national leaders.

Spiritually speaking, enough seed has been sown to bring millions to Christ! There is no fault in the seed. The problem is water. The extent of the harvest can depend upon the amount of prayer that waters the seed.

Your prayers can help cultivate the crop. Jesus warned that the trouble, persecution, worries of this life, and deceitfulness of wealth would cause some to drop by the wayside and become unfruitful (see Matt. 13:20-22). Your prayers can encourage, strengthen, and protect the germinated seed during the critical period when new life comes up.

Your prayer actually can influence world leaders and activate the resources of God! Proverbs 21:1 says, *"The king's heart is like channels of water in the hand of the Lord; He turns it like a watercourse wherever He wishes."* Join with Ezra, Nehemiah, Esther, Deborah, and Daniel—whose prayers changed the heart of rulers, altered the laws of the land, and influenced national leaders.

PRAYING FOR THE HARVEST

I have a friend named Dick Simmons who is one of the overlooked key intercessory people in this nation. More than 35 years ago, Dick was attending Bible college in New York City. He was marked for intercession. In the middle of the night on the bank of the Hudson River, he began to cry out to the Lord in intercession for New York City. He prayed at the top of his lungs, "Lord, I beseech Thee that You send forth laborers unto Your field!" His agonized prayers were so loud at 2:00 A.M. (even by New York City standards!) that he suddenly was bathed in floodlights on the riverbank. Cautious police officers shouted out, "What are you doing? You have been reported for disturbing the peace because you've been waking up people!"

Dick bellowed back, "Oh, I am just praying to the Lord of the harvest that He would send forth laborers into His field."

The police officers must have been shocked, or else they agreed with Brother Simmons. They let him go without any charges or warning. That very night, the Holy Spirit of God descended on a little skinny preacher in rural Pennsylvania and gave him a divine call to take the gospel to New York City. Do you know his name? It was David Wilkerson. It is no wonder that when David Wilkerson established the first Teen Challenge Center in New York City, he chose Dick Simmons to be its first director.

I tell you the truth: If you dare to echo the prayers of Jesus, your petition will pierce the heavens and the Father Himself will receive it. Then, as the bowls of prayer are tipped over, He will send it hurtling back at the speed of light to the earth to effect His divine will and judgment on the matter! Study God's Word and learn how to pray with power and effectiveness. Begin to pray the tenfold claim of the Colossians in Colossians 1:9-12:

> *For this reason also, since the day we heard of it, we have not ceased to pray for you and to ask that you may be filled with the knowledge of His will in all spiritual wisdom and understanding, so that you may walk in a manner worthy of the Lord, to please Him in all respects, bearing fruit in every good work and increasing in the knowledge of God; strengthened with all power, according to His glorious might, for the attaining of all steadfastness and patience; joyously giving thanks to the Father, who has qualified us to share in the inheritance of the saints in light (Colossians 1:9-12).*

117

WISDOM APPLICATIONS

Dick Eastman lists five claims of revelation and five claims of blessing in this passage from his book, *Love on Its Knees*, which I've adapted for this chapter:[7]

Five Claims of Revelation

1. Pray for a revelation of *God's will* for the gospel worker, a person, or people. This prayer is for divine direction.

2. Pray for a revelation of *God's wisdom*, or divine perception. This is a prayer that the person would not only be filled with the knowledge of God's will, but that he or she would also know *how to implement* it in a wise manner.

3. Pray for a revelation of *God's understanding* or comprehension. This means that the person will know what the Father has for him or her to do and how to do it—as well as when, where, and with whom.

4. Pray for a revelation of *God's holiness* so the person will walk worthy of the Lord and please Him in every way.

5. Pray for a revelation of *God's pleasure* or divine gratification. This is really key. You need to pray for this for your own life and for the lives of those whom God has laid on your heart. Pray that they would have a revelation of the pleasure God finds in them and their work of obedience. Also pray for Jesus to become their chief pleasure. In reality, this is a prayer for intimacy.

Five Claims of Blessing

1. Pray for *increased effectiveness*, productivity, and fruitfulness. Pray that the persons will become more fruitful in every good work and deed.

2. Pray for their *increased devotional growth* or spirituality. Pray that they might know Him and draw near to Him in increased intimacy.

3. Pray for an *increase of strength*. You could call this "increased durability," where the worker or person will have a thick skin like a rhinoceros, but with a tender heart.

4. Pray for an *increase of patience*.

5. Pray for an *increase of joy*. Pray that they will have an increased delight in the work of the Lord. Ask God to bless them and pray for a bucket of joy to be dumped on their heads. The joy of the Lord is our strength (see Neh. 8:10).

How Will the Harvest Come?

The great harvest of the Lord never will be accomplished by a few hired hands, nor even by a team of highly gifted evangelists, apostles, prophets, teachers, and pastors. The work is too great, the scope too grand to be accomplished by an elite few—only a praying Church can harvest an entire lost world in one generation! God is calling every member of His household back to the foundation of prayer that launches every great move of God in the earth. It is time for us to hit our knees and pray the heart of God into being in the earth! It's time for us to recapture our marbles and have the mind of Christ concerning the "House of Prayer for All Nations."

I know prayer changes things! Therefore, I pray to the Lord of the Harvest that He send forth laborers into the fields as they are already white unto harvest. I want to see people from every tribe and ethnic group before the throne of God, ao I ask you, Father, that you burden my heart with a nation, a people and tribe so that I can be a co-laborer with you for the great End Time harvest! Awesome! Amen and Amen!

Endnotes

1. Strong's, **worship** (#4352).

2. Strong's, **prayer** (#8605).

3. *Theological Wordbook of the Old Testament,* Vol. 2, **prayer** (*lepilla,* Hebrew #1776a), 725-726, provides the descriptive words noted in my text, although I have not quoted directly from this reference work.

4. Tarr, "A Prayer Meeting."

5. "The World of 1732," *Christian History*, Vol. I, No. 1 (Worcester, MA, 1982), 13.

6. Dick Eastman, *Love on Its Knees* (Grand Rapids, MI: Chosen Books, 1989), 105. Selected statistics and data were drawn from this excellent book on prayer and the harvest.

7. Eastman, *Love.*

CHAPTER 8

Restoring the Expectation
of the Supernatural

The old priest's hands trembled as they slowly dropped finely ground bits of freshly mixed incense on the ancient altar of incense in Herod's temple. *How many times have I entered this place and done this very same thing before the Presence?* old Zacharias asked himself. The haunting sound of the unceasing chants, moans, and cries of the people praying outside the Holy Place could still be heard, even though several feet of solid stone walls and the thick veil of separation had dulled their force in part.

Reciting ancient intercessory prayers from the Torah dating back to Moshe (Moses), Zacharias the priest felt a strange thrill rush through his body as a thought long forgotten rose unbidden to his mind: *Why don't you ask for yourself?* Taking the last pinch of incense in his right hand, he gently dropped it into the flickering flames of the smoking fire on the altar and whispered to the Presence he could almost feel through the thick veil:

"O Holy God of Abraham, Isaac, and Jacob, from birth I have been called Zacharias, 'Yah has remembered,' and my lovely Elizabeth has been called 'God of the Oath' or 'the oath of God';

yet the name we hear the most is 'barren.' Would You remember me, Ancient One, though I have no heir? You have declared You would bless those who seek You, and I seek You this day. Grant me my heart's desire that we may praise and worship You in the company of a son before we die. Then our very names will declare the truth and mercy in Thy name, Holy One."[1]

Suddenly, the dim flickering light from the seven flames of the golden candlestick in the Holy Place were eclipsed by a blinding light and a paralyzing sense of awe. As Zacharias suddenly spun around to see where the light came from, he had a sinking feeling in the pit of his stomach. *I'm a dead man!* he thought. *I've transgressed against the Almighty and am undone....* The moment his eyes stopped on the brilliant figure standing to the side of the altar of incense, he was nearly overcome with terror and fear.

> *But the angel said to him, "Do not be afraid, Zacharias, for your petition has been heard, and your wife Elizabeth will bear you a son, and you will give him the name John. You will have joy and gladness, and many will rejoice at his birth"* (Luke 1:13b-14 NASB).

Moments later, old Zacharias staggered out of the Holy Place trembling and rubbing his eyes with tears soaking his priestly robes. The other priests rushed to him and peppered him with urgent questions about what had happened and why he had been gone so long. They soon realized that the priest they had known most of their lives was a changed man. God must have visited him in the Holy Place, because he could no longer speak. Some thought that Zacharias had been cursed for a transgression of some kind and figured he was lucky just to be alive, but others who knew him well thought differently.

In time, they would all know exactly what had happened in the Holy Place that day. The truth is that in that intimate scheme of the old, represented by the trappings of priestly worship with bloody sacrifice, fire, and temporary atonement, God had birthed the new. Gabriel, the archangel of God, met Zacharias in the Holy Place and announced God's answer to his fervent prayer, but the priest's unbelief caused him to lose his ability to talk.

It was Elizabeth, whose name literally means "the oath of God," who would carry God's promised son in her aged womb for nine months from the time Zacharias returned home. She mysteriously disappeared from public view for the first five months, and many of the gossipers in the city swore she was trying to escape the public ridicule that had met her everyday at the markets and even during the temple gatherings on holy days.

Zacharias would not and could not speak for nine long months after his supernatural encounter. But on the eighth day after the miraculous birth of his son, John, the first words the aged priest uttered as he gazed on the new life destined to prepare the way for eternal life were words of worship and praise to God (see Luke 1:64). Zacharias's supernatural encounter with Gabriel is a wonderful picture of the way God intervenes in the affairs of men.

*Those of us who are filled with **His** desire and **His** secrets find ourselves launched on a journey of supernatural encounters, intercession, and intervention as we speak forth the decrees of God in the earth by His Spirit!*

Zacharias began the process with a dedicated, consecrated life that was blameless in God's sight. He stood in the office of priest offering sacrifices of prayer and praise to God on behalf of others, to the accompaniment of corporate prayer and intercession. He finally asked God to act on his behalf, and the fruit of his prayer became a blessing to all the world and every generation afterward. He didn't realize that his secret heart's desire had been God's desire all along. His petition—bathed in worship and praise and carried to the heart of God in personal and corporate prayer—caused the ancient seed of God, His Word and promises, to be planted in the earth as a new seed of supernatural intervention to be revealed in the fullness of time.

THE KISS OF GOD ON OUR HEARTS

God longs to see us linger before Him and offer the incense of prayer and praise on the fire of our passion for Him. If we do, we will soon find our hearts filled with the very desires and secrets of God. Those of us who are filled with *His* desire and *His* secrets find ourselves launched on a journey of supernatural encounters, intercession, and intervention as we speak forth the decrees of God in the earth by His Spirit! We can literally blend the power of the unchanging Ancient of Days with the faith He gives us today to create something new and holy in the earth. What a privilege we have in our ability to pray in Jesus' name!

THEN IT HAPPENED!

The wind was blowing fiercely outside our house just before midnight on October 6, 1992. It was the Day of Atonement, the ancient day of sacrifice, salvation, and new beginnings observed by Jews around the world for thousands of years. At 11:59 P.M., I was suddenly awakened by a crash of lightning that brightly illuminated our bedroom. In the eerie flickering light in our backyard I saw a man standing in our room. He looked straight at me.

I blinked and looked at him again, and he continued to look at me for what seemed like the longest minute of my life. Then I heard the words, "Watch your wife. I'm about to speak to her." Michal Ann was still asleep when the being spoke to me, but when the clock reached the midnight hour, the manifested *appearance* seemed to leave the room. I could sense the being's presence although I could no longer see him. Michal Ann instantly woke up, and trembling in the fear of the Lord, I whispered to her, "An angel has just come!" Together we shook in the bed with the covers pulled up right to our faces for the next 30 minutes. Tyler, our four-year-old son, had moved to our room when he had become frightened by the storm, and he was asleep on the floor on my side of the bed through the whole ordeal. For some reason, I floated off to sleep for a while without telling Michal Ann what the "man" had said. She was now left wide awake as the sense of the presence increased and I slumbered away.

While I slept, the Holy Spirit began to move upon Michal Ann in some rather unusual ways. At one point she felt a hand in the middle of her back exerting great pressure, and she heard herself moaning and groaning as the activity increased. It was so intense that she was afraid to even look at herself in the mirror, thinking she might discover that her hair had turned white or the appearance of her face had been dramatically rearranged. Just as this portion of the intense encounter came to an end, I woke up again. A light was shining over our bedroom dresser. We continued to tremble as the fear of the Lord was ever so strong. We tossed up a feeble prayer and said, "Lord, if this visitation is of You, then cause one of our children to have a dream about an angel to confirm this visitation." We waited and quietly prayed, "Oh God, oh God, oh God!" I think we identified with the old gospel hymn, "Were You There?" in the line where it says, "Sometimes He causes me to tremble, tremble, tremble." I then fell asleep for the rest of the night, but Michal Ann was left alone again until 5:00 A.M. with God's terrifying presence thick in the room.

Later that morning we awakened to find Tyler standing right beside me, and he said, "I had a dream last night that an angel come and visited our house." Justin, our firstborn, was asleep in his room right above us on the second floor. He was all excited that morning when he told us that he, too, had a dream that angels had come. In the dream he was shown a white horse that was being prepared for a mission that was yet to come. Interesting, huh? Michal Ann was shown the same horse when at one point she seemed to have been "taken up in the Spirit." How comforting and reassuring this was! God was watching over His Word to perform it. Remember, when something is truly of the Lord, He will confirm it by the witness of two and three.

A Dream Beforehand

Although we were somewhat already versed in the supernatural activities of the Holy Spirit, this was a totally new league. But it's interesting to note that in the summer of 1992, I had a dream in which the Lord instructed me to study the ministry and function of angels. I avidly read all the Scriptures on the subject and every book that I could find. I thought it was an interesting assignment, but I had no idea that in the fall of that year our household would become a "visitation ground" for angels. Nor would I have guessed that for the following nine weeks the visitations would center primarily around my wife. At this point, you'll have to hear the rest of the story from Michal Ann herself:

> I heard a spiritual song in my sleep that I just couldn't figure out. It bothered me so much that I woke up. The singer in this dream sang, "Where is my bride, oh my God?" I pondered those words over and over until I finally realized that it was Jesus who was singing the song.

> I was getting some clarity on some of the issues brought up by the Holy Spirit at that point, but it was very overwhelming. I didn't know what to do with the song, and this really bothered me because I felt that it had much to do with Jesus' return to claim His spotless Bride, the Church.

> The problem is that as a Bride we don't know what we should look like, and we don't really know what our Groom looks like either. He is coming, *and we don't intimately know who He is!* I felt a deep burden to search out His face and to *know Him* just for His sake. As if in answer to my quest, the Lord sent angelic visitors into our bedroom night after night for the next nine weeks, and each time they came, they ushered in the manifest presence of God. This weighty glory of God was almost unbearable to me. I was scared out of my wits because the fear of the Lord was so intense.

> One time I saw several fireballs literally arch through the room and hit me squarely in the chest. Their impact electrified my body and made me wonder if I was going to survive the experience. Before the arrival of the Presence each night, I would earnestly pray to experience God's fullness again. As His glory filled my bedroom, I would feel the pressing weight of His holiness and begin to cry out, "Please Lord, I can't take anymore! I think I am going to die!"

Finally, the Lord said, "Ann, do you want Me to come or not?" I took several days to think over this question because I was just so overwhelmed by the intensity of His presence.

In His mercy, the Lord brought me to a place where I had to decide what really mattered the most to me. He was no longer willing to let me just waffle back and forth from day to day and retreat into my excuses and fears. Perhaps it was a form of the "Mount Moriah" test and God wanted to see if I was willing to climb upon the altar of God myself as a living sacrifice. Finally, the Lord confronted me with a choice—not a choice between salvation or damnation, for I was already forgiven and saved since a child— but a choice to make between what I had already experienced and what God longed yet to impart to me. The problem was that He wanted me to empty my hands before He filled them with something greater. He asked me, "Well, what do you want?"

Finally, I responded to Him in the way He always wanted me to respond. I said, "Well, Lord, if I live, I live; and if I die, I die. But I really, really want You to come." Angelic visitors continued to visit our bedroom regularly. They still visit on occasion. In every case, they always speak of the things that are nearest and dearest to the heart of God. At times we are struck with ecstasy, and at other times we become struck low with the fear of God and a stark revelation of our sinfulness compared to His incomparable holiness and beauty.

I came out of these times of visitation with a burden to help men and women get ready for His coming—His intimate, personal coming. Every time that I hear some of the songs we sing with in- credible words and melodies about intimacy with God, I tremble. When we sing, "Oh Lord, let me feel the kisses of Your mouth; let me feel Your warm embrace, feel the tenderness of Your touch..." and the like, I'm convinced experientially that *we have no idea what His kiss is like!*

Just as I pulled back when the manifest presence of God entered my room with unexpected results, we as a corporate body of believers often recoil when He really answers our sung prayers and touches us with His glory and fire! We back up and say, "No! You're coming too close." Meanwhile, God is saying, "Do you realize that all of those songs you've been singing to Me are arousing My love? I am coming to you and you don't even know that it's Me."

"I felt a deep burden to search out His face and to know Him just for His sake. As if in answer to my quest, the Lord sent angelic visitors into our bedroom night after night for the next nine weeks, and each time they came, they would usher in the manifest presence of God. This weighty glory of God was almost unbearable to me."
—Michal Ann Goll

Changed by His Presence

After the most intense period of these angelic visitations had passed, I walked into our kitchen one night, looked at Michal Ann, and said, "I just don't know who you are anymore." She looked at me and replied, *"I just don't know who I am becoming."* Since then, I've seen a new depth of raw power and spiritual authority rise up in Michal Ann's life. God imparted something to her that allows her to see past the barriers of fear, and she is able to minister security, hope, and destiny with authority. Even people who have never known Michal Ann before recognize that someone or something incredible has totally transformed her into a mighty woman and minister of God. This highlights one of the most dynamic roles of supernatural encounters in our lives.

PRESENCE EVANGELISM

What does this subject of "Restoring the Expectation of the Supernatural" have to do with the lost art of intercession and the great harvest? Everything! Once again, I want to share a supernatural experience my wife had in which the Lord demonstrated to her *one of His ways* of winning the lost to Christ. She told me about a series of dreams that she had concerning the Lord's desire to touch the Jewish people. She saw herself standing beside me. We were facing three very tall Jewish men with black beards and heavy hair. Their arms were folded, and they were looking sternly at Michal Ann as if to say in judgment, "Who do you think you are that God would use *you* to bring the gospel to the Jews?"

Michal Ann remembers looking at these men and saying, "You are absolutely right. I am nobody. There isn't a reason in the world why God should choose me. It is only by the anointing of the Lord that we can do anything." Then she began to turn the conversation away from the men and toward the Lord. Then she began to cry out to the Lord with words the Lord gave her to say: "Release Your anointing, Lord! Release Your presence and Your Spirit so that revelation will come and the blinders will fall off of their eyes."

In this dream, a spotlight suddenly shone from Heaven upon Michal Ann. Immediately the three critical men were all struck by the light. Instantly, they lifted their hands to their mouths and took a step back. Then they began to declare, "I see!" The favor of the Lord had been released and a major turning point had been reached. Where the Jewish men had been closed to the gospel before they saw the light, now they were suddenly open to receive the truth about the Messiah.

Michal Ann told me that she felt like she is walking down a path of discovery—not just with ministry to the Jewish people, but in the whole ministry field:

> It's almost like that is my life story. I feel like God looked down from Heaven and picked the most unlikely, insecure, fearful person for the job.

It doesn't depend on the person; it depends on God and His in-filling power. That's the only way that I can do anything, go anywhere, or have any anointing. When Jim and I first began to travel together, he would speak and then he would call people up for ministry. I dreaded it because he would always turn to me and say: "Okay, Ann, you start over on that side and I'll start over here."

"In my case, God shined His light on me said,
'I choose you!' He didn't ask for my opinion
or the opinion of anyone else on the matter."

—Michal Ann Goll

I used to feel like a duck out of water. I didn't know what to do. I felt so awkward that I just wanted to evaporate down into a little puddle and go underneath the door so nobody would notice that I had slipped out. I would try to pray, and I'd watch Jim to see what he was doing, but it just fell flat. You know what? God wasn't upset by that at all. He wasn't upset at making me uncomfortable or putting the spotlight on me. He allowed me time to become secure in Him.

This should bring hope to every person, regardless of gender, race, or age. It doesn't depend on us—it depends on the Lord alone. When you adjust the way you operate to accommodate this truth, then you can do things, and God can use you in any way that He sees fit. All you have to do is make yourself available. In my case, God shined His light on me said, "I choose *you!*" He didn't ask for my opinion or the opinion of anyone else on the matter.

I watched the Lord impart to Michal Ann a supernatural grace, favor, and anointing to do His bidding. In fact, He has come to both of us in ways that we wouldn't even know how to ask for.

THE PURPOSE OF THE SUPERNATURAL

Why do we need to restore the "expectation of supernatural encounters"? One reason is found in Ephesians 6:12, which says, *"For our struggle is not against flesh and blood, but against the rulers, against the powers, against the world forces of this darkness, against the spiritual forces of wickedness in the heavenly places."* When you face a supernatural adversary, you *must* defeat him by supernatural means. The illusory weapons of the flesh and physical realm mean nothing to spirit beings—whether they are holy or unholy.

The second reason is that in every true revival in human history, evidence of signs and wonders confirm the Word that was preached. These "signs following" were a beacon to the unsaved declaring that God is alive and well. He is still in the soul-saving, miracle-working business. *"And they went forth, and preached every where, the Lord working with them, and confirming the Word with signs following. Amen"* (Mark 16:20 KJV).

The third reason has to do with the nature of God who is Spirit, and the ordained purpose of God's most powerful and mysterious servants, the angels. By definition, it is impossible for our supernatural God who is Spirit to step into our death-bound, flesh-dominated world apart from supernatural means. That is why liberal theologians around the world work so hard to disprove and cast aside every reference to the supernatural in the Bible; they fear the idea that God is truly God and that He intervenes supernaturally in the affairs of men and women. Such a God is totally uncontrollable and even unpredictable! This is totally unacceptable to professional religious scholars who have never personally encountered the supernatural God.

Let me briefly outline the three primary functions and at least fifteen activities of angels (for more on this subject read my wife's and my co-authored book *God Encounters*) involved in the affairs of God and man:

Three Primary Functions of Angels

1. They continually offer praise and worship to God.

   Praise Him, all His angels; praise Him, all His hosts! (Psalm 148:2).

   Let them praise the name of the Lord, for He commanded and they were created (Psalm 148:5).

2. They are sent as "flames of fire" and "winds of God" to minister to mankind.

   And of the angels He says, "Who makes His angels winds, and His ministers a flame of fire" (Hebrews 1:7).

   Are they not all ministering spirits, sent out to render service for the sake of those who will inherit salvation? (Hebrews 1:14).

3. Angels were created to excel in strength and obey the voice of His Word so they could perform God's Word.

   Bless the Lord, you His angels, mighty in strength, who perform His Word, obeying the voice of His Word! Bless the Lord, all you His hosts, you who serve Him, doing His will (Psalm 103:20-21).

Types of Angelic Activities

1. They minister the presence of the Lord (see Isa. 63:9; Rev. 18:1).

2. They are messengers sent to pronounce God's will (see Matt. 1:20; 2:13,19; 28:1-7; Luke 1:19,26).

3. They release understanding in dreams and visions (see Dan. 8:15-19; 9:23; Rev. 1:1).

4. They help give guidance and direction (see Acts 8:26; 27:23-24,29; Gen. 24:7,40).

5. They bring deliverance (see 2 Kings 19:35; Isa. 37:36).

6. They provide protection (see Ps. 34:7; 91:11-12; Matt. 18:10).

7. They are present upon the death of the saints (see Ps. 23:4; 116:15; Luke 16:22; Jude 9).

8. They release strength (see Dan. 10:16-18; Matt. 4:11; Luke 22:43).

9. They are used as healing instruments in the hands of God (see John 5:4).

10. They continually offer praise and worship to God (see Gen. 32:1-2; Luke 2:14; Rev. 5:11-12).

11. They bind demonic powers at God's bidding (see Dan. 10:13; Rev. 12:7; 20:1-3).

12. They serve as divine watchers (see Dan. 4:13,17; Acts 12:20-23; 1 Tim. 5:21).

13. They help reap many of the harvests of God (see Matt. 13:39-42; 24:31; Rev. 14:6,14-19).

14. They execute the judgments of God (see Gen. 19:11; Exod. 12:18-30; 2 Kings 19:35; Acts 12:20-23; Rev. 16:17).

Our interactions with angels hinge on five basic premises:

1. **We are coworkers with Christ**, and as such, God's resources are released by man's invitation in accordance with His will. Intercession releases angelic intervention.

2. **Answered prayers influence or help to determine the destiny of individuals and nations.**

3. **There is an innumerable company of angels waiting to be dispatched** (unemployed angels, if you will). *"As the host of Heaven cannot be counted, and the sand of the sea cannot be measured"* (Jer. 33:22a).

4. **Angels are involved in virtually all of the everyday, practical affairs of men.** They are involved in virtually every facet of everyday life and the normal activities of mankind.

5. **Angels are often utilized by God to deliver or execute His answers to our prayers.**

ANGELIC INTERVENTION THROUGH INTERCESSION

Many examples of angelic intervention stand out in the Bible. Abraham interceded for Sodom and Gomorrah and held back judgment until Lot's family could be saved by angelic couriers (see Gen. 19:1-29). Daniel persisted in intercession until the angel Gabriel, himself, arrived after battling the dark prince of Persia on behalf of Daniel and the Jewish people (see Dan. 10:12-21).

The New Testament record also tells us about three different instances where prayer and the supernatural intervention of angels led to the deliverance of early Church disciples from prison. Peter, the apostle, was personally escorted out of an impregnable prison by an angel dispatched in response to the single-hearted prayers of the saints in Jerusalem in Acts 12:7-10.

> *So Peter was kept in the prison, but prayer for him was being made fervently by the church to God. And on the very night when Herod was about to bring him forward, Peter was sleeping between two soldiers, bound with two chains; and guards in front of the door were watching over the prison. And behold, an angel of the Lord suddenly appeared, and a light shone in the cell; and he struck Peter's side and roused him, saying, "Get up quickly." And the chains fell off his hands* (Acts 12:5-7).

In this instance, it was *prayer* that delivered Peter from Herod's murderous schemes (see Acts 12:5). The fervent unified prayers of the 120 believers waiting for the coming of the Holy Spirit nearly a year earlier had caused the place to be swept with wind and fire in Acts 2:2-6. Then, beginning in Acts 16:26, the sacrificial praise and worship that Paul and Silas offered from their stocks in the prison at Jerusalem triggered a violent earthquake and angelic deliverance for them!

I've already described the vision received by Evald Rucky, the Moravian pastor from the Czech Republic, who saw angels going back and forth between Heaven and earth in response to the prayer of the saints. We've also examined my family's experiences with angelic visitors in the night. You probably think these stories are pretty exciting, but you may automatically exempt yourself from such "special experiences." Don't.

We are about to move into another phase in the powerful move of God on the earth. We've experienced a "second Pentecost," if you will, characterized by the new wine of joy and refreshing that swept through churches across the world. Then the Lord stepped up the pace and ignited the fires of repentance, cleansing, and holiness when He suddenly descended on the Father's Day service at Brownsville Assembly of God in Pensacola, Florida. Now we are entering into a third level characterized by *power*.

I WILL RESTORE PENTECOST

In this third wave, the Holy Spirit will be utilizing the gift of workings of miracles throughout the Body of Christ. The Lord told me before all of this began, "I will restore Pentecost." The advent of the Holy Spirit on Pentecost was marked by three signs: the wind of the Spirit's coming; the fire of the holiness and purity of God indwelling believers; and the intoxicating effect of the wine of the Spirit on mankind.

The first phase of God's appearing fell on Toronto in 1994. Several prophetic statesmen described it by saying, "God was serving the appetizer." The Spirit of God fell on Pensacola in 1995 with holy fire that restored the fear of the Lord (and the corresponding understanding of His immeasurable grace) to the Church. Now, we are going deeper. In September of 1996, on the Day of

---

We've feasted on the wine of the Spirit and have been refreshed with laughter, joy, and renewal. We have bowed our knees in humility and repentance under the fiery presence of our jealous God, the righteous King of glory. We have been lifted up in His grace as righteous, holy, and pure in His sight. Now, we are about to experience the wind of God, characterized by powerful supernatural gifts, supernatural encounters, and angelic intervention!

Atonement, the Holy Spirit whispered this word to me: "Tell My people not to treat this current move of refreshing as an American fad. Tell them they must stay with it long enough until it crests, until the next wave comes."

I believe for the past decade and even longer, we have been experiencing a "Pentecost experience" marked by the same three signs seen in the Book of Acts, but in reverse order. We've feasted on the wine of the Spirit and have been refreshed with laughter, joy, and renewal. We have bowed our knees in humility and repentance under the fiery presence of our jealous God, the righteous King of glory. We have been lifted up in His grace as righteous, holy, and pure in His sight. Now, we are about to experience an unprecedented *wind of God*, characterized by powerful supernatural gifts, supernatural encounters, and angelic intervention!

I believe that we are to be praying down supernatural encounters on a large scale. Already, some are seeing incredible divine interventions on the mission field in answer to prayer. In his article, "Praying Down Miracles," Bruce Steinbaum wrote:

> *Researchers contend that 80 percent of the new Christians in South Asia come to Christ as a direct result of some kind of supernatural encounter.* Church planters among the Gamit people of Gujarat, India, say that membership jumped from 0 to 600,000 in ten years as a result of hundreds of miraculous healings.[2]

Mr. Steinbaum also reported in the same article that in Saudi Arabia, some Christian nurses were asked to pray for a 13-year-old girl who was dying of leukemia. According to sources familiar with her story, the girl was visited by the Lord Jesus one night, even though she knew nothing about Jesus. The next day, she announced to her astonished parent that she had met her Healer, and the entire family is now following Christ. We need to pray down supernatural encounters for cancer patients like this little girl. Pray that God will visit those who are dying of terminal diseases and will heal them. Pray that entire families and villages will follow God because of testimonies to divine visitations from on high. Steinbaum also writes:

The gospel has even penetrated Islam's holiest city! In 1993, several Saudi believers conducted a prayer march around the periphery of Mecca, the site of the annual Hajj, or pilgrimage. They asked God to establish a church in the city and reveal Himself to the two million truth-seeking pilgrims who visit the city every year to pay homage to Allah at the Ka'bah shrine. According to at least two sources, Jesus made a special guest appearance at the 1994 Hajj, declaring to a group of Nigerian Muslims that He indeed was the One they were seeking.

Some Kurds reportedly have come to Christ as a result of intercessory prayer and supernatural dreams and visions. [The Kurds live in an area some people call Kurdistan, situated in northern Iraq.] One of these new Christians was converted a few years ago in Turkish Kurdistan. An avowed atheist and the editor of an influential Marxist magazine, this man was arrested in 1981. A Christian who gave him a New Testament prayed that Jesus would reveal Himself to him in a series of dreams. At their next meeting, the man became a Christian and announced that Jesus is the One who cleanses sins.

In Tunis, as in other parts of the Arab world, God is employing dreams, visions, and miraculous healings to draw truth-seekers to Himself. One dramatic example of this phenomenon involved a group of the Sufi Muslims in northern Africa who were chanting and dancing before Allah in hopes that he might reveal himself. They say that Jesus appeared and declared that He is the true God.

According to the missionaries in the region, many other people living in the isolated reaches of the Sahara Desert have reported similar visions of the Lord—and they are requesting Scriptures so they can learn more about Christ.

In Egypt, a Moslem military official said he was visited by Jesus Christ in a dream. Upon waking, he immediately sought out

Christians in his unit to see if they could provide him with a copy of God's Word. Finding only one believer in his officer corps, he quietly asked if he could borrow the man's Bible. In a manner reminiscent of Ananias' reluctant ministry to Saul of Tarsus, the Christian cautiously agreed. And after several days of poring over the Gospels, the officer became a disciple of Jesus. According to reports out of Cairo, this man has become a bold witness.

A team of Christians reported that a Pakistani Moslem recently had a dream about a Bible descending out of Heaven. While he gazed at the book in amazement, the man said he heard the voice of Jesus declaring, "This is My Word—obey it." Similar reports of dreams and visions are commonplace inside Pakistan.

In Cuba a divine visitation of healing descended upon a small town about 40 miles outside the capital. Everyone who walked into the church there was healed. As news of this spread, people from all the other towns began arriving. They too were healed. Eventually people from all over the island were coming and being healed. This went on for six weeks. Tens of thousands were saved. Many churches were planted and interest in the gospel rose nationwide because everyone had heard the news. It was so powerful that even the Communist government could not deny these events. (Most of these healings were by laying on of hands—in a *Methodist* church.)[3]

REMEMBER, WHAT GOES UP, MUST COME DOWN!

Let me ask *you* the question that God asked me in the Czech Republic in January of 1993: *Have you ever considered the multidirectional dimension of prayer?* The only way souls are saved, the sick are healed, demons are cast out, churches are established, and the explosive supernatural gifts of God are unleashed is for people to pray. God is once again driving home this simple but vital component to true revival:

If we want to restore the expectation of the supernatural, then we must first restore the labor of love through fervent prayer on our knees! It was no accident that the Moravian believers enjoyed such effectiveness in their missionary work—they lived by one motto that we need to adopt as our own in the Church: "No one works unless someone prays." Supernatural encounters are commonplace among praying people, and myths among the prayerless. It is time for the redeemed nation of kings and priests to don their linen robes and enter the Most Holy Place to offer prayers, petitions, and intercession for all men. It is time to unleash the power of God Almighty on the earth through unleashed prayer to Heaven.

FROM THE EYES OF A CHILD

Let me close out this chapter by telling you another story centering around our oldest son, Justin, when he was only seven years old. In February of 1991, I was in Atlanta, Georgia, on an intercessory mission of prayer concerning what would later be called the Gulf War. Months before the conflict ever broke out, the Lord had spoken to me to be a man of prayer through the month of February. So I kept my schedule clear to have concentrated time to be before the Lord. While I was away, Justin had an encounter of supernatural dimensions.

He was lying awake in the top bunk of his bed late one night when with his eyes he saw clouds enveloping his room. A brilliant throne appeared to be established in the midst of the clouds, and some creature-like things with wings, full of something that looked like fish scales, surrounded the throne. They each had different faces, and seven-year-old Justin said that one had the face of an eagle, another looked like a bull, a third looked like a lion, and the fourth had the face of a man.

A ladder descended into his room and angels traipsed down the ladder—carrying fire in their hands. Single file, they would descend one at a time, stand in the room, and then proceed back up the ladder, only for another to be released to do the same. The last angel to come carried a piece of paper in his hand, and he left it on Justin's dresser. This angel climbed back up the ladder; the ladder ascended into the clouds; the clouds enfolded the throne; then everything seemed to vanish to the natural eye. Only one thing remained. A piece of angelic stationery was yet visible on Justin's dresser with a few short words imprinted upon it. Justin must have looked puzzled when he read the note. Guess what it said: *Pray for your dad*. Amazing, isn't it? God even wants children to expect supernatural results when they pray!

EXPECT GREAT THINGS FROM GOD

Prayer releases Heaven's arsenal to come to the aid of man. Why not expect a supernatural God—who has not changed—to move in extraordinary ways? Who knows, when the Almighty receives the incense of your prayers, maybe a whole troupe of angels will be sent forth in response to your invitation bidding His will! Why not expect great things from God in answer to your prayers?

I believe that the supernatural is for today! In fact, I want to see demonstration of God's great power through my life! Use my prayer life to release angels on assignment. Open my spiritual eyes to see in the spirit realm! I want to be a believing believer and see Heaven come down to earth. As for me and my house, we shall pray down supernatural encounters for the glory of God!

ENDNOTES

1. This prayer, of course, is a *fictional account* of what Zacharias the priest might have said, since according to Luke 1:13 we know he had made a personal petition to the Lord. It seems likely this priest would want to make the petition from the most advantageous place at the most appropriate time—what better time under the Old Covenant than with the final offering of incense before the veil shielding the ark of the Lord and within earshot of continuous intercession from the congregation of the Lord?

2. Bruce Steinbaum, "Praying Down Miracles," an article included in the training notebook, *Fire on the Altar*, compiled and published by Jim Goll of Ministry to the Nations (Nashville, TN, 1995).

3. Steinbaum, "Praying Down."

CHAPTER 9

Restoring the ATM
(Apostolic Team Ministry)

"It's time for the 'A Team' to come forth!"

"It's time for the ATM."

"It will be apostolic, authentic, abandoned Christianity."

"It will be telescopic—with prophets looking down the telescope of time and evangelists telling the good news. And it will be microscopic with pastors and administrators caring for the house."

This word came to me in a dream in the summer of 1996. I knew that this promise was that these three ministries (apostolic, telescopic, and microscopic) would cooperate together and not compete. In my heart, I thought, *Now that would be a dream!*

As I awakened from this dream, I saw a vision of a man using an ATM (automatic teller machine) card at a bank machine and receiving a withdrawal of funds. Perhaps the Lord was saying that Apostolic Team Ministry will be used to release great supplies from His storehouse for the last days' ministry. One thing is for certain at this writing: New teams and new streams are emerging every day. It is time for the prophetic to come into maturity and for true, authentic, humble, apostolic ministry to emerge.

While I was in Austria ministering at a School of the Prophetic in August of 1996, the Holy Spirit awakened me in the night. I heard His external audible voice, saying:

> "For the next 38-1/2 months, I will light up one city per month with My sustained presence—like Toronto and Pensacola."

I knew in my spirit that this word of the Lord was global in scope, and that these cities would be distributed all over the world. I also knew that some of these cities would be in out-of-the-way places, and that some of these outpourings would not be publicized widely. The names of a number of mostly unfamiliar cities in foreign countries came to mind at the same time. As I pondered the words I'd heard, I realized that the time period given in the word would end somewhere on the Day of Atonement in 1999. (Now I am not predicting the second coming of Christ, the mark of the beast, or any such thing. I simply am relaying a powerful encounter to stir your faith into action.) Perhaps cities filled with spiritual fire are part of God's strategy for the harvest.

THE POWER OF SUSTAINED PRAYER

I believe that everything we have experienced to this point is but a foretaste of what God is bringing to the Church! Up to this point, we have witnessed historic worldwide prayer events that revealed the great power of unity in prayer to God. Yet, what God revealed to our small group of intercessors on the Moravian watchtower in February of 1993 is that He is raising up *sustained unity, sustained prayer,* and *sustained intercession* in a simple pattern and style that He raised up years ago at Herrnhut. The question is obvious: If 300 people conducting sustained prayer in twos and threes for more than a century turned the world upside down 200 years ago, what can *millions* of anointed intercessors accomplish through sustained prayer in the presence of God?

Unfortunately, much of the Church has been limping along with blind eyes and crutches when it should be running to the battle! Most church congregations in the Christian world have squandered away their potential by living under the illusion that the two vital leadership gifts listed in Ephesians 4—the apostle and the prophet—somehow "passed away" somewhere between the conclusion of the Book of Acts and our day.

Gifted teachers and pastors have kept us well fed and content to learn and leave—often with little accountability for applying our ever-growing wealth of knowledge. Wise pastors brought in evangelists as often as possible and gave them orders to comfort the afflicted and afflict the comfortable, but the first love of an evangelist is on a stage or tree stump somewhere surrounded by seas of *unsaved* faces. Without the strength, foundation, and visionary leadership of apostolic ministry, our churches have lived in a perpetual state of weakness in insecurity. Deprived of the prophetic insight and God-given sense of spiritual direction and correction found in the prophet, the Church has been stumbling from one short-term goal to another, never really having or perceiving God's will for the corporate Body. Remember, where there is no vision, the people perish (see Prov. 29:18).

THE CHURCH'S CONDITION

As a result, the Church has resembled a person whose diet is limited exclusively to heavy starch-based or fat-rich foods and sweets. The Church has become bloated from feasting exclusively on the fruits of "pastor trees" and "teacher trees," with just enough spice from rare helpings of "evangelist trees" to provide occasional heartburn. In other words, our ignorance has deprived our corporate Body of two of the five "God-ordained daily allowances" of spiritual nutrients necessary to produce a healthy, productive, and completely equipped and spotless Bride. We are weak and malnourished because of an incomplete and unhealthy balance in our spiritual diet!

God has examined the modern-day global Body of Christ and, particularly, the North American Church, and He has found her wanting, much as He did with the churches in the Book of Revelation. She is bloated, given to much sleep and slumber, and she dislikes exercise or "the work of the ministry" in many forms. Her members have a track record of avoiding anything that requires time, effort, or personal accountability for *doing* what God commands in His Word.

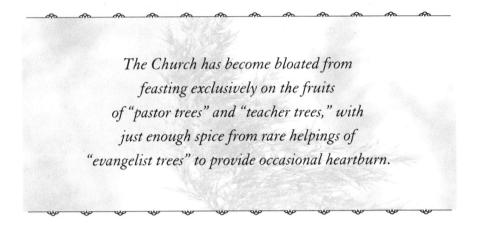

The Church has become bloated from feasting exclusively on the fruits of "pastor trees" and "teacher trees," with just enough spice from rare helpings of "evangelist trees" to provide occasional heartburn.

"IN TEN YEARS"

Now let me review some of our prophetic history. In April of 1984, a friend of mine, revivalist Mike Bickle, heard the voice of the Lord say something like this: "I am going to begin a new work in the earth in ten years." God commissioned him to call forth intercessory prayer in a sustained manner over the next decade and beyond. That wasn't exactly the kind of word he wanted to hear because he had just planted a new work. He was an energetic pastor in his late twenties. He didn't really want to wait ten years for a major move of God and spend much of the time in a room simply reminding God of His word, but he had no choice. God also told Mike that He was speaking to a prophetic gentleman named Bob Jones and instructed Mike to contact the man. When they met and compared notes, they discovered that God had spoken complementary things to both men at the same time while in two different locations! Their insights became like two pieces of an interlocking puzzle.

The Lord gave Bob a revelation at that time about the Bible account of Joseph's stay in Pharaoh's prison. He told Bob that it was a parable of what was going to occur over the next decade. Since God's Word declares, *"Surely the Lord God does nothing unless He reveals His secret counsel to His servants the prophets"* (Amos 3:7), it is appropriate for me to summarize Bob Jones's prophecy released in mid-1984. When Joseph was wrongfully thrown into Pharaoh's prison for refusing the advances of Potiphar's wife, he shared his confinement with Pharaoh's butler and baker, who had both been thrown in jail for offending him. Each man had a dream and Joseph accurately interpreted their dreams and predicted what would happen over the next three days.

The butler was restored to Pharaoh's good favor with all of the rights and privileges of his position of service. He was released to serve in the king's presence. The baker, however, was hung high for all to see and beheaded. The birds of the air feasted on his flesh because he had served his bread with hypocrisy. (In other words, he said one thing and did another. You can stop squirming now.)

Bob Jones's revelation was that the Lord was going to deal with the hypocritical bakers in the Kingdom, as well as with the teaching or "table" ministries in His house. He was going to deal with His household in a severe manner to cleanse the leaven of hypocrisy from our teaching ministries. At the end of these ten years, after the Lord's dealings, new little unknown servants, butlers of the king, would be released to serve at the table of the Lord and be given the awesome responsibility to serve the new wine and living bread in the King's presence. (I believe this word actually goes far beyond a single ten-year period. It describes the ongoing and progressive cleansing work of the Holy Spirit in our day and in past Church history.)

A DRAMATIC FULFILLMENT

Not long after this prophecy was released, something dramatic occurred that shocked the entire church community and outraged unsaved people around the world. Jim and Tammy Bakker were formally indicted for fraud. Many other unsavory activities also were exposed publicly at their sprawling ministry in Fort Mills, South Carolina. The greatest, most damaging exposures concerned blatant hypocrisy involving money, sexual activities, and extravagant lifestyles that brought shame to ministry and the Christian world. I only mention these things for instruction and verification of Bob Jones's prophecy, not to point a finger or be critical of anyone. God knows, we each need His mercy.

The exposure and public punishment of the Bakkers became symbolic of the cleansing work that God was doing throughout the Church. The ten years have gone, and this cleansing still continues. But something new entered the picture in early 1994 when God poured out His Spirit on a small church at the end of an airport runway in Toronto, Canada, and many other places. A new wine was being poured out as the Lord began to release His little servants to serve new wine and living bread in the King's presence once again.

Another landmark sign came exactly at the end of the ten-year period prophesied by so many vessels of God: Jimmy Bakker was released from prison. That, in itself, was a prophetic proclamation that the Lord intends to restore backsliders to the "pool of His purpose." During this same period of time, the Holy Spirit gave me some insight. One afternoon, I was watching our children playing on our swing set in our backyard. Suddenly, I saw an open vision superimposed over the natural scene. With this extra dimension of spirit-sight activated, I saw a grown adult man sliding down our slide; he was positioned on his back, headfirst. In this vision, the man slid into a round swimming pool at the base of the kids' slide. I lifted up an instant request, "What does this mean?"

Immediately, a reply came within, "I will restore the backslidden man into the pool of My purpose." One of the first signs that a great harvest is coming and has come upon us is that the prodigals are coming home from every quarter. I rejoice to see Jim Bakker a restored man of humility among a people of restoration, once again proclaiming the mercy and grace of Jesus Christ. Let the prodigals return.

In the 1980s, many prophetic voices prophesied about a coming grand revival, still yet to come: "And the stadiums will be filled; a faceless generation (little servants) will come forth. Jesus will be magnified as the stadiums are filled as healings, miracles, and the dead are raised." This speaks of a rapid, large-scale revival and harvest that only can be described as a Great Awakening in our land. In the 1980s, it took a lot of courage to release a prophecy like that. Today, it is easier because we have already seen people lining up at 4:00 in the morning just to attend evening revival services in various places

One of the first signs that a great harvest is coming and has come upon us is that the prodigals are coming home from every quarter.

and continents around the world. But a *tidal wave* of God's presence is about to break forth.

When God unleashed His Spirit in January of 1994, it was like a "cork" had popped out of a bottle. New wine began gushing forth all over God's people. I was ministering with my intercessory coworker, David Fitzpatrick, in a conference in Indianapolis, Indiana, in September, the day after the Day of Atonement that same year, when God began to speak to me. What I heard there relates closely to the events that occurred during this ten-year period of cleansing.

"IT'S TIME TO BEGIN"

I was asleep and alone in a totally dark room when I was awakened by the audible voice of the Lord. It was an unusual experience. It seemed like an angel had blown a trumpet that resonated in the room and woke me up. I sat up immediately in the bed and felt what I can only describe as "the presence of destiny" in my room. A large angel now stood at the end of my bed. The digital clock read 2:02. I sat in the bed immersed in the tangible presence of destiny for the next 30 minutes. But I had been awakened by hearing these words: "It's time to begin."

The angel was what you might consider a "typical looking" angel that was dressed in white with wings, and I could see hands under the wings. The hand under one wing emerged holding a green cup filled with fresh oil. (I thought it was wonderful because it instantly brought to mind Psalm 92:10, which says, *"But Your have exalted my horn like that of the wild ox; I have been anointed with fresh oil."*

The Lord is dispensing fresh oil in our day. If you are stale and in need, ask Him to pour some of His anointing oil on top of you right now. Just express your hunger, desire, and need as you declare, "Over here, Lord! Right now. Remember me."

As I watched the angel holding the green cup filled with oil, he suddenly went "Shhhhoooo" and left the room. I then looked over in the corner of the room and saw a bottle sitting there. The really odd part was the label on the bottle that said, "Crisco Oil." My mind was really working at this point, and though I didn't say anything out loud, I was thinking, *Oh God, why do You always do this? Why does the prophetic always have to have this parabolic edge to it?*

Suddenly I "saw the light" and said to myself, *Oh, now I see: Jesus Christ, the **Christos**, the Anointed One.* God was saying that the anointing represented by the oil wasn't being given to only one man—it was to the *Cristos company*, the "ChrisCo." He was releasing His oil for a whole company of people to come forth in His power and glory.

It's time for a kingdom of faithful butlers to arise. It is time for the cups of oil borne about in the green vessels symbolic of the priestly tribe of Levites—meaning His intercessory people, His people of praise, the people of His brilliant presence—to arise and come forth conquering and to conquer.

I continued to gaze at this green bottle of oil that was about 12 to 18 inches tall—and at the scores of angels who began to fly out to unknown destinations. Some bore cups of the oil of anointing, others carried bottles of new wine, and all of them made the same sounds, "Shhhooo, shhhhoooo," before they departed. This visitation lasted about a half an hour.

Experience has taught me not to overlook any detail in a vision—even the minor and seemingly inconsequential points. I asked the Lord, "What is the 202 about?" This was the time, 2:02, on the face of the digital clock when the visitation began. He dropped into my mind the Song of Solomon and the Book of Revelation. I turned on the light and opened my Bible to read, *"Like a lily among the thorns, so is my darling..."* (Song 2:2) and the passage in Revelation 2:2 praising the Ephesian church for its deeds, for its toil and perseverance, and for its test to determine false apostles.

The gifts of God operating apart from the character of God are a prescription for catastrophe. God, though, is taking care of that through the cleansing and pruning periods. Now we were being freshly called back into service—hopefully wiser, humbler, and purer than we were before our affliction.

This reminded me of the grueling ten-year period so many believers had endured in a "dry land." He had finally brought forth the cure for the spiritual boredom that had settled into the Church. He was calling us back to His royal banqueting table and bringing His butlers, His little servants, cups overflowing with the oil of gladness and anointing, priestly bottles of new wine and the joy and refreshing of the Lord.

RECEIVING GOD'S APPRAISAL

While many believers (including myself) felt at times that we were barely "hanging on by our fingernails," the Lord had a different perspective. He is well aware of the desert conditions we endured, but He says to those who have hung on and continued, "I bless you for your godly perseverance. I say unto you that you are My lily amongst the thorns. You are My darling, My Bride." Now He is releasing fresh bottles of wine and the fresh anointing of His great presence upon us.

The four little words that I received from an audible voice that day simply declared: "It's time to begin." After I'd pondered those words for several months, I began to see that God had, somewhat, put us on a "pause" mode because, as a Church, our depth of character simply didn't match up with our level of giftedness. The gifts of God operating apart from the character of God are a prescription for catastrophe. God, though, is taking care of that through the cleansing and pruning periods. Now we were being freshly called back into service—hopefully wiser, humbler, and purer than we were before our affliction.

After that time, I was given a dream in which I saw a painter like Michelangelo painting the arm of the Lord coming down out of clouds. Then I saw the hand and arm of a man rise up from earth. The two were about to touch each other. I noticed a "baton" in the hand of the Lord as His arm extended toward earth from Heaven. I realized that the Lord was placing this baton in the hand of man as he extended his arm toward Heaven. The baton represented four "heart standards" given to Mike Bickle in a separate prophetic revelation, and to many others as well. These four heart standards were:

1. Day and night prayer.

2. Extravagant giving.

3. Holiness of heart.

4. Unwavering (or prevailing) faith.

This dream illustrated God's longing to entrust once again into the hands of His people heart strands of purity and devotion, outreach and mercy. Now these promises have never been promised or released to just one body, one city, one denomination, or even to one "stream" in the Body of Christ. These are foundational principles and promises and prophetic declarations of the heart of God for the whole Church, the Body of Christ. God was declaring to us after a long drought, "I will restore day and night prayer. I will restore extravagant giving. I will restore a people of purity and holiness of heart. And I will restore prevailing faith amongst My people."

THE ARM OF THE LORD

I began to search the Scriptures for references to "the arm of the Lord" and discovered some key passages:

...You shall well remember what the Lord your God did to Pharaoh and to all Egypt: the great trials which your eyes saw and the signs and the wonders and the mighty hand and the outstretched arm by which the Lord your God brought you out (Deuteronomy 7:18-19a).

Yet they are Your people, even Your inheritance, whom You have brought out by Your great power and by Your outstretched arm (Deuteronomy 9:29).

And know this day that I am not speaking with your sons whom have not known and who have not seen the discipline of the Lord your God—His greatness, His mighty hand, and His outstretched arm, and His signs, and His works, which He did in the midst of Egypt to Pharaoh the king of Egypt and to all his land (Deuteronomy 11:2).

And the Lord brought us up out of Egypt with a mighty hand and an outstretched arm and with great terror and with signs and wonders (Deuteronomy 26:8).

For by their own sword they did not possess the land; and their own arm did not save them; but Your right hand, and Your arm, and the light of Your presence, for You did favor them (Psalm 44:3).

And the Lord will cause His voice of authority to be heard. And the descending of His arm to be seen in a fierce anger and in the flame of a consuming fire, in a cloudburst, downpour, and hailstones (Isaiah 30:30).

It appears that whenever the "arm of the Lord" reaches into our time-space world that it has something to do with signs and wonders, with deliverance, and with the brilliant display of God's power. Isaiah 52:10 tells us, *"The Lord has bared His holy arm."* What is the purpose of His presence, and what is the purpose of the prophetic gifts? Isaiah 52:10 says, *"In the sight of all the nations, that all the ends of the earth may see the salvation of our God."*

> *Who has believed our message? And to whom has the arm of the Lord been revealed?* (Isaiah 53:1)

> *I have made the earth, the men and the beasts which are on the face of the earth by My great power and by My outstretched arm, and I will give it to the one who is pleasing in My sight* (Jeremiah 27:5).

The "arm of the Lord" symbolically represents strength and power, the demonstration of God's right to both discipline and deliver in the Scriptures. During a time of extended ministry in the Los Angeles area, I went with Lou Engle, the pastor of prayer at Harvest Rock Church in Pasadena, California at that time, and some other friends on an expedition to do some on-site locational praying. We prayed at the original site of the Azusa Street outpouring and also at the little house nearby where the Holy Spirit first baptized believers before the little group moved to the Azusa Street location. Then we headed for a place called Pisgah, which was another center of Pentecostal renewal.

CALLING FORTH THE ARM OF THE LORD

Finally, we visited Angelos Temple, the founding church of the Four Square International Church established by Aimee Semple McPherson in the 1920s. That church and Aimee Semple McPherson's ministry were very powerful in that day. After we went through a little museum area and examined some of the documents on display, our wonderful host took our party of eight right into the auditorium to pray.

Once we reached the auditorium and settled in to pray, our host left us alone in that incredible place. We saw a beautiful grand piano sitting on the platform. Someone mentioned that Aimee Semple McPherson played it during her services. At that point, my dear missionary friend, Marcus Young from Thailand, sat down at the piano and began to play in the spirit.

Then, we just waited quietly in the presence of the Lord in this wonderful auditorium that had played host and witness to countless miracles, signs, and wonders in this century.

While we waited on the Lord, I sat down on a step leading to the platform, just soaking in the sweet presence of the Lord in that place. Finally, I just lay down on the platform before the presence of the Lord. When we first came in, we were struck by the perfect acoustics of the auditorium. It had a high-domed ceiling. You could speak from the stage without a microphone, and the sound resonated around the building with total clarity.

While Marcus played on the piano, I began to pray out loud as I basked in God's presence. Then I *really* began to pray. Finally, I began then to prophesy as something started to rise up within me. I moved into a place of prophetic declaration and began to prophesy:

> I will restore the sacred altar. I will restore My fire upon My altar. I will restore. I am going to bring forth the arm of the Lord. I am going to release apostolic restoration ministries. I am going to restore the four faces of My gospel. I am going to release the four faces of My living creatures that are around My throne. Let the arm of the Lord come forth!

Then I prophesied the restoration of the four-square gospel of the King, the Savior, the Baptizer, and the Healer; and of the ARM—the Apostolic Restoration Ministries. It is time for the apostolic restoration ministries to begin.

THE PROPHETIC SETS THE TABLE

It has been prophesied for years that the prophetic would set a table for the apostolic. I must declare boldly that it is time to begin. I am not giving definitions of what the "apostolic" is in this book; that is not my purpose for this particular book. Nevertheless, it is time for apostolic restoration ministries to come forth.

I continued to pray, prophesy, and release prophetic declarations. Finally I said out loud, "Oh, may the altar of the Lord be restored!" Suddenly, I felt the floor start to rise underneath me out of the floor! No, I wasn't having a dream or vision, and I wasn't in a trance. An altar began to rise out of the floor that must have measured three feet wide by six feet long. It kept rising, and I kept prophesying: "The altar of the Lord is coming. Fire is coming on My altar." (I'm telling you a prophetic event that really happened.)

A LIVING SACRIFICE

I couldn't help but notice the significance of my position on the rising altar while I prophesied life and restoration. God is looking for living sacrifices according to Romans 12:1: *"...present your bodies a living and holy sacrifice, acceptable to God, which is your spiritual service of worship"* (Rom. 12:1b). *We* are the sacrifice that is well pleasing and acceptable in God's sight. He is jealous for us, and He wants us to present our whole being on His altar—with spirit, soul, and body.

When the altar reached the end of its track, I just kind of slid down slowly until the altar was right behind me, as other people in the group watched. I remained in that place declaring in prophetic proclamation:

> I will restore the fame of My great name in all the earth. I will restore the four faces of the gospel. I will restore My truth of being Savior, Baptizer, and Healer. I will release My four faces and My living creatures. I will bring forth, and I shall roll up My sleeve, and I shall bare My holy right arm. I will restore the ancient altar. I will bring forth My holy right arm.

Things will probably end up looking different from what we expect right now, but the Lord is going to breathe fresh prophetic and apostolic teaching and revelation on the ancient discipline of day and night prayer. He is going to release a new understanding of extravagant giving and a new place of holiness of heart. The fire of God is an all-consuming fire that can dry up cancer or convict men of their sins.

APOSTOLIC RESTORATION MINISTRIES

What is the arm of the Lord? It is a symbol of the Lord's strength and power. It is the demonstration of God's ability to both discipline and deliver.

It is likely that His arm refers to apostolic restoration ministries or apostolic team ministries in this great revival. But even more accurately, the arm of the Lord usually refers to Jesus Christ Himself: "And I will bare My holy right arm." You know, this is not about us. It isn't about anointed men and women. This is all about Jesus—the Sacrificial Lamb receiving the reward of His suffering. Let's make our focus clear.

This is not about us. This is about our wonderful Messiah, Jesus Christ, our transcendent Majesty.

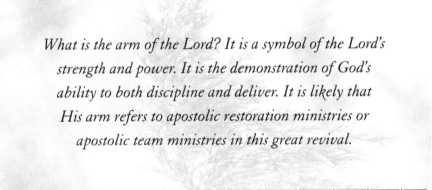

What is the arm of the Lord? It is a symbol of the Lord's strength and power. It is the demonstration of God's ability to both discipline and deliver. It is likely that His arm refers to apostolic restoration ministries or apostolic team ministries in this great revival.

This is about the power of His great presence. If you recall, I mentioned how God once told me, "I am going to teach you to release the highest weapon of spiritual warfare. I am going to teach you to release the brilliance of My great presence." What is the highest weapon of spiritual warfare? Why, it's God Himself.

The Lord has been looking for broken people. He has been looking for a humble people who can be trusted with God's treasure because they know that it's not them—it is Jesus. According to Psalm 110:2, the Lord is seeking them out to place His scepter of kingly authority and power into their hands to rule over their enemies out of Zion (God's abiding presence). Let the "A team" come forth. Let the arm of the Lord be stretched out! It's time for a faceless people to emerge, a generation of little butlers whose passion is the exaltation of this one Man, God and King—Christ Jesus, the Lord.

I declare it is time for the ATM – for apostolic team ministry to begin! Use me! I want to see authentic, apostolic Christianity cover the earth as the waters cover the seas. I declare, "It is time to begin the greatest show on earth! It's time for another great awakening. Let it start here. Let it start now in Jesus great name!" Amen

CHAPTER 10

The Day of the Watch Has Come

"I will restore the ancient tool, the Watch of the Lord, that has been used and will be used again to change the expression of Christianity across the face of the earth."

This final chapter of this section represents the most difficult task of this book. Why? Because a burden has been placed on my heart to break the vile curse that has overcome and contaminated the Church and the ministry since the days when James echoed the teachings of Jesus and admonished believers:

But prove yourselves **doers** *of the Word, and not* **merely hearers** *who delude themselves. For if anyone is a hearer of the Word and not a doer, he is like a man who looks at his natural face in a mirror; for once he has looked at himself and gone away, he has immediately* **forgotten what kind of person he was** (James 1:22-24).

Some years have passed since the Lord told me, "It is time to begin." Since then the fire of God has fallen in countless places across the globe (including supposedly "impregnable" places such as Japan and Mecca). My burden is to awaken the "saved and redeemed" and remind them *who they are!* Only then will they begin to obey and, in turn, pray for the salvation of the lost in God's great harvest. Oddly enough, this has often proven to be the most difficult group to reach!

Since God ignited my burden for the Watch of the Lord at Herrnhut, the site of the great Moravian prayer watch, it is no accident that He has sent me to draw from their deep pool of wisdom again and again along my journey. The Day of the Watch has come. The words of the Rev. John Greenfield, the great Moravian evangelist and author, ring as true today as they did 70 or more years ago:

> Prayer always precedes Pentecost. The Book of Acts describes many outpourings of the Holy Spirit, but never apart from prayer. In our own day the great Welsh and Korean revivals were preceded by months, if not years, of importunate and united praying. Hence the supreme importance of the prayer meeting, for it is "the power house of the Church."[1]

In previous chapters, I mentioned that the Lord told me, "I will restore Pentecost." Many people think that is an odd or even heretical statement. "After all, Pentecost happened once and for all." I also spoke of a "Second Pentecost" coming to the land, but while I was completing some research for this final chapter, I discovered a better way to describe this work of God: He is sending yet *another* Pentecost!

The Moravians, and many supposedly "fundamental evangelical" leaders believed and prayed for the same thing and received it! The only way to spread fire is to catch fire! Theology never saved anyone—only a personal experience with a living Savior can do that. Theology never launched a worldwide revival. In every case, it took a fresh revelation of the living Savior to ignite the world with fire from Heaven. Before you can participate in the Watch of the Lord, you must offer yourself as a living sacrifice on the altar of God and let Him baptize you afresh in His holy fire!

D.L. Moody, one of America's most revered evangelists and conservative church leaders, had this to say about the Holy Spirit in one of the last sermons he preached in his life:

> See how He came on the day of Pentecost! It is not carnal to pray that He may come again and that the place be shaken. I believe Pentecost was but a specimen day. I think the Church has made this woeful mistake that Pentecost was a miracle never to be repeated. I have thought too that Pentecost was a miracle that is not to be repeated. I believe now if we looked on Pentecost as a specimen day and began to pray, we should have the old Pentecostal fire here in Boston.[2]

God is restoring the fire of the Holy Spirit to His people so *we* will restore the fire of prayer on His altar of incense and release the glory of God on the earth! Look at the striking parallels between the outpouring of the Holy Spirit on people of prayer in Jerusalem, and on another people of prayer 17 centuries later in Herrnhut, Saxony!

> Verily the history of the Moravian Church confirms the doctrine of the great American evangelist [D.L. Moody] as to the need and possibility of the baptism with the Holy Ghost. The spiritual experiences of the Moravian Brethren two centuries ago bear a striking resemblance to the Pentecostal power and results in the days of the Apostles.
>
> The company of believers both at Jerusalem and Herrnhut numbered fewer than three hundred souls. Both congregations were, humanly speaking, totally devoid of worldly influence, wisdom, power and wealth. Their enemies called them "unlearned and ignorant." Their best friend described them in the following language:
>
> *"Ye see your calling, brethren, how that not many wise men after the flesh, not many mighty, not many noble are called; but God hath chosen the foolish things of the world to confound the wise, and God hath chosen the weak things of the world to confound the things which are*

mighty; and the base things of the world, and things which are despised, hath God chosen, yea, and things which are not, to bring to naught things that are, that no flesh should glory in His presence" (1 Cor. 1:26-28).

On both these small and weak congregations God poured out His Holy Spirit and endued them with power from on high. At once these believers, naturally timid and fearful, were transformed into flaming evangelists. Supernatural knowledge and power seemed to possess them. "Mouth and wisdom" were given them which "none of their adversaries were able to gainsay or resist."[3]

The same God who engineered the miracles in Jerusalem and in Herrnhut in the 1700s appears determined to do the same across the earth before the dawn of the millennium! God is not interested in "corporate assent" to the principle of revival—He demands personal surrender, commitment, and sold-out service in prayer and public witness to His glory!

When the people of God dare to surrender to the Holy Spirit of God and then live lives of continuous consecrated prayer, they will display an infectious joy that will draw the lost to them again and again in divine appointments of destiny. An editorial in the *Wachovia Moravian* described a "typical Moravian" affected by the Pentecostal outpouring of that day:

There was a Countess several generations ago who had led what the world calls a very merry life. She was highly situated in society, connected in close friendship with kings and emperors and princes. She was a welcome centre on brilliant occasions of dance and festivity in view of her brilliant gifts and witty conversation, and yet she became afflicted with an incurable melancholy. None of her amusements and recreations satisfied her any longer and everything before her and around her seemed dark indeed.

Under the old custom of measuring shoes for the feet of their wearers, a humble Moravian shoemaker was one day invited into her presence. As he opened the door, she was struck by the remarkable cheerfulness which shone forth from his face. She watched him closely while he knelt at his humble task of measuring for the shoes and was deeply impressed by the unaffected happiness written upon his very looks. She was led to say to him, "You seem to be a very happy man." "Yes," he said, "I am very happy all the time." "You are very different from me," the highborn lady said. "I am just as miserable as anybody could be. Would you mind telling me what makes you so happy?" "No," the Moravian shoemaker said, "I'll be glad to tell you. Jesus has forgiven my sins. He forgives me every day and He loves me and that makes me happy through all the hours."

The job was finished and the man went away. But the Countess thought over what he said. Thought led to prayer and prayer to conviction and conviction swiftly introduced her into a joyful faith in the shoemaker's Saviour. She became a witness for Christ among titled people and especially at the court of the Emperor of Russia, Alexander I, her intimate friend.[4]

GOD'S INTENTION

Matthew Henry wrote, "When God intends great mercy for His people, the first thing He does is to set them a-praying."[5] God intends to cover the earth with His glory and with a flood of mercy and grace. But first God must wake His sleeping giant, the Church. It is time for you and I to shake the world for Christ from our places of prevailing prayer! We can no longer afford to hear the urgent word of the Lord and walk away passively. The call is the same regardless of what title or flavor adorns the sign over the door of our place of worship.

I am compelled in the spirit to urge you to prayer. After I ministered a message on "The Watch of the Lord" in Mobile, Alabama, I returned home to discover that I had been sent a very beautiful framed picture in the mail. This gracious giver had no idea what effect that picture would have on my life. I personally believe that this picture constitutes *the highest prophetic word* that I have ever been given in my life! It is a picture of monumental proportions in front of my eyes.

The picture depicts a great city encircled by a protective wall. A hill rises on one side and coming over that hill are hundreds of invaders on horses. The picture also depicts a watchman on the wall—*a watchman who has fallen asleep.* The trumpet normally used to signal the approach of danger lays useless beside the slumbering watchman. Meanwhile, the enemy draws closer and closer to the defenseless city.

When I first unwrapped this picture, I thought, *Lord, this is wonderful. This is a great gift.* Then I read the verse inscribed below the scene, and suddenly I wasn't as excited as before. The verse was Ezekiel 33:6, which says, *"But if the watchman sees the sword coming and does not blow the trumpet, and the people are not warned, and a sword comes and takes a person from them, he is taken away in his iniquity;* ***but his blood I will require from the watchman's hand."***

I avoid using this Scripture passage in a legalistic or condemning manner, but it made the "sobriety of God" sink into my inner being. I know that I am called to be a watchman of the Lord. I don't want to fulfill the failure depicted in that picture. Jesus warned us 11 times to "be on the watch, be on the alert, wake up, and watch out that no one deceives you." Too many of us have stopped listening and stopped caring.

God is calling His watchmen—every blood-washed saint and redeemed king and priest—in groups of twos or threes to come together on the wall.

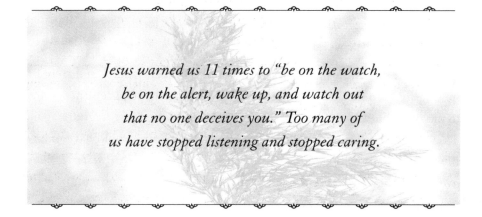

Jesus warned us 11 times to "be on the watch, be on the alert, wake up, and watch out that no one deceives you." Too many of us have stopped listening and stopped caring.

He is calling forth the ancient tools to bring salvation to our generation. *Do you believe dead men's bones can live again?*

I believe dead men's bones *will* live again. I believe that the same Spirit who kept the promises of God for generations in the past is waiting for us to enter into the Holy of Holies for our time and our generation! There is only one path for you to take if you have received and believed the message of this book: You need to be possessed. (Don't close your mind and the pages of this book—this is a Bible concept!) God wants you to be possessed with His Spirit in the same way Gideon was! The Amplified Bible says:

> But the Spirit of the Lord clothed Gideon with Himself and took possession of him, and he blew a trumpet, and [the clan of] Abiezer was gathered to him (Judges 6:34 AMP).

GET POSSESSED!

God is waiting for a people to get possessed. He wants a people who will literally be clothed with God Himself, and will blow the trumpet with holy boldness as watchmen on the wall. Are you willing to be possessed? Are you ready for a radical change of clothes?

I have always liked Gideon because I can really identify with him. He was minding his own business and working in his own field when somebody (an angel of the Lord) tapped him on the shoulder and said, "Hey you, mighty man of courage, God wants to use you."

I can imagine Gideon looking around and saying, "Who in the world are you talking to, buddy?" (See Judges 6:11-17.) As it was with Gideon, God's analysis of our potential is vastly different from our own. God is looking for a people who understand how small they are and how great He is. Then, He just loves to turn the tables on all the naysayers and contenders by possessing us and taking residence within us.

Gideon's father was not a righteous man because he had built up the high places in honor of idols and false gods. Everyone nearby came to the site to conduct their devilish rites of idolatry. In the same way, our nation can no longer be called a "Christian nation" because we've turned aside to the idols of self, personal pleasure, and rebellion. Nevertheless, the Spirit of the Lord gave Gideon the task of tearing down the very high places that his father had built! Gideon decided to obey the angel's command, but he was wondering, *I'm not quite so sure because you're talking about dividing my own household here.* He was so afraid of his father's reaction to the destruction of the high places that he did it at night.

Gideon's clumsy attempt to hide his deed didn't work, evidently because one of the ten men who helped him decided to tell all (see Judg. 6:29). When the angry idol worshipers confronted Gideon's father, Joash, he said prophetically, "If *he* [Baal] *is a god, let him contend for himself because someone has torn down his altar*" (Judg. 6:31b). Although Joash intended for this statement to be a curse on the guilty man, it set up a test of truth similar to the confrontation of Elijah with the priests of Baal when God's fire consumed all of the priests of Baal as well as Elijah's water-soaked altar and sacrifice. In the ancient traditions of that day, it was understood that anyone who dared to break the curse would themselves receive a penalty in their own lives.

Gideon faced some serious problems that day. You may be facing some obstacles in your life that make commitment to the Lord's call seem impossible or even suicidal. The Lord is looking tirelessly for a people who will overcome small mentalities, insecurities, and fears to allow Him to take control. When you allow God to clothe you with Himself, when you "put on Christ," you will have a totally different perspective of the obstacles challenging you today. Too many Christians are afraid to step out of their own comfort zones and venture into places that the world (and many Christians) call "too radical."

GOD'S REWARD SYSTEM

God has a reward for people who dare to step out on the limb of faith and just keep on going. There was a reward for Gideon. He counted the cost of obeying God's command. He had to face his paralyzing fear of reprisal if he dared to come against his own father's household. Gideon counted the cost and stepped over the line into obedience to God anyway. He was still "human" enough to do the deed in the dark of night, but the point is that he obeyed. Once he stepped out, the Bible says he "waxed strong." He became stronger!

Look what happens to the man who steps forward for "more" of God in his life. The Bible says, *"So the Spirit of the Lord came upon Gideon; and he blew a trumpet, and the Abiezrites were called together to follow him"* (Judg. 6:34).

I was in a prayer conference in Canada several years ago after I had spent three solid months seeking God. Many of those days were spent praying in tongues for four to six hours a day. This trip to Canada was my "first time out" after three months of prayer. I went into a place of intercession there in Canada, and the Holy Spirit illuminated this verse in Judges chapter 6. He put on my heart to read the passage from the Amplified Version.

As usual when I go into intercession and travail, I was sitting on the floor of the room. When I turned to Judges 6:34 in my wife's Amplified Bible, I read these words with astonishment: *"But the Spirit of the Lord **clothed Gideon with Himself and took possession of him**, and he blew a trumpet, and [the clan of] Abiezer was gathered to him* (Judg. 6:34 AMP).

I've got a word from the Lord for you: *Be possessed*. We hear a lot of talk about people being possessed by the devil, but I have something shocking to tell you: *God is looking for a people that He can possess*. He wants to do more than legally own us because He purchased us with His blood. He also wants to experientially *have us*. I don't know about you, but I want to be possessed

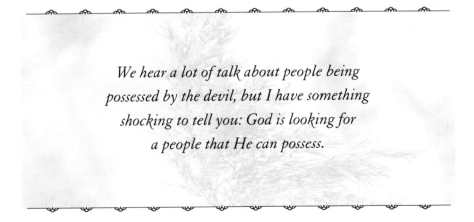

We hear a lot of talk about people being possessed by the devil, but I have something shocking to tell you: God is looking for a people that He can possess.

by and with God. I want literally to be clothed with Him. I urge you to let God come upon you, to be possessed of God.

Look at the evidence in the Bible. When the Spirit of the Lord came upon or possessed Gideon, he was changed into a new man! He was no longer just a little puny guy with a mouth full of excuses about how poor his tribe was. He was possessed by God. He dared to sound the trumpet and, suddenly, to his surprise, thousands of people were suddenly willing to follow him! One moment he's a farmer in a barley field. The next moment he gets possessed by God and sees 32,000 armed men come at his simple command ready for a battle to the death with the Midianites who held the Jews in slavery! That must have been some day.

MAKING THE TEAM!

God's work of transformation didn't stop there. He was out to raise up a true leader, not just a one-time, soon-to-be-forgotten hero. When God came down to examine Gideon's newly found troops, He told Gideon, "Hey, buddy, there are too many of them out there. In fact, there are so many of them coming with you that *if you win*, the men will look at themselves and say, 'We did it.' "

And the Lord said to Gideon, "The people who are with you are too many for Me to give Midian into their hands, lest Israel become boastful, saying, 'My own power has delivered me.' Now therefore come, proclaim in the hearing of the people, saying, 'Whoever is afraid and trembling, let him return and depart from Mount Gilead.'" So 22,000 people returned, but 10,000 remained (Judges 7:2-3).

This scene was similar to the public basketball tryouts for the Los Angeles Lakers or Chicago Bulls basketball teams. A whole bunch of people answered Gideon's call, but only one-third of them made the first cut for people who were fearful and afraid. Over two-thirds of Gideon's miracle crowd left. (This statistical percentage probably would hold true today.)

Then the Lord said to Gideon, "The people are still too many; bring them down to the water and I will test them for you there. Therefore it shall be that he of whom I say to you, 'This one shall go with you,'

166

he shall go with you; but everyone of whom I say to you, 'This one shall not go with you,' he shall not go." So he brought the people down to the water. And the Lord said to Gideon, "You shall separate everyone who laps the water with his tongue, as a dog laps, as well as everyone who kneels to drink." Now the number of those who lapped, putting their hand to their mouth, was 300 men; but all the rest of the people kneeled to drink water (Judges 7:4-6).

Twenty-two thousand of Gideon's surprise helpers were afraid. That's easy to understand. That left him with 10,000 armed men for the battle. Then came "Cut number two." God said, "Send them down to the river for a drink of water. And Gideon, I want you to watch them while they do it. Whoever gets down on both knees, send him home. But whoever laps the water like a dog, keep him. I can run with them."

I wonder if Gideon thought something like, *Sure, God, yeah, right*. It doesn't matter because Gideon's actions spoke louder. He sent 10,000 armed men stampeding down to the river for a drink, and 9,700 of these football-player types got down on both knees and put their faces down into the water to really go for it. The problem was that when these guys were down on both knees with half of their faces in the water, the only thing that they could see was their own reflection. Less than one man out of every ten made this final cut, leaving Gideon with only 300 out of his original instant army of 32,000 men. He felt good about it, though, because these men met God's main requirement for battle fitness: "Look for those who will lap the water like a dog."

I don't know if you have ever watched a dog eat or drink, but dogs always *watch* while they eat or drink. They keep one eye on the water bowl and one eye on the terrain to see who is approaching. A dog doesn't bury himself in self-containment. To me it sounds just like the message of Jesus in the Gospels. Four times He told us, "Do not be afraid" (that's the first cut). Four times He said, "Endure, stand" (that's the second cut). A full 11 times the Lord commanded us: "Watch" (the final and most important requirement for battle).

NEHEMIAH'S TOOLS

When Nehemiah the prophet risked all to rebuild the wall of Jerusalem in occupied territory filled with violent enemies, the first thing he did was to establish watchmen on the walls. In fact, everyone who worked on the wall was both workman and watchman, builder and soldier. They would work with a trowel in one hand and a spear in the other.

God is quickly setting things into place to build His Church in a quick work. Again, this building project takes place in temporarily occupied territory surrounded by violent and desperate enemies. The first thing God is setting in place is "the Watch of the Lord." You've made the first two "cuts." Now He has led you to the river for a test. Will you look at yourself, at what you have, and be content with what you see? Or will you eagerly receive His gifts today but carefully keep a watch for the Master's signals and the enemy's schemes?

What are the rewards for these labors? If you could ask the Moravians this question, they would instantly answer: "To win for the Lamb that was slain the reward of His sufferings." The prayers of the "possessed" are more powerful than any of us know. A German historian named Dr. Warneck wrote in his book, *Protestant Missions*, "This small Church [the Moravians] in twenty years *called into being* more missions than the whole Evangelical Church has done in two centuries."[6]

The work of the Holy Spirit was so complete and deep in the people at Herrnhut that they literally began to live out in microcosm the plan of God for His spotless Bride when He returns! Listen to the words John Wesley wrote after visiting Herrnhut in August of 1738, as recorded by Moravian historian Rev. John Greenfield:

> "God has given me at length," he wrote to his brother Samuel, "the desire of my heart. I am with a Church whose conversation is in Heaven; in whom is the mind that was in Christ, and who so walk as He walked." In his journal he wrote: "I would gladly have spent my life here; but my Master called me to labour in another part of His vineyard. O when shall this Christianity cover the earth, as the waters cover the sea?"[7]

ON A WORLDWIDE SCALE

God fully intends to do on a worldwide scale what He did more than 200 years ago among a divided group of believers from diverse backgrounds. He is out to raise up a Church, a nation of kings and priests, whose determination is to know nothing among men save Jesus Christ and Him crucified, whose theology has become Christology, and whose creed was in one word, the "Cross."

Are you willing to be "possessed for prayer"? Will you yield yourself as a living sacrifice this very day so that God can clothe you with Himself and conduct warfare for souls? Little keys open big doors. What goes up must come down!

The key to fulfillment and fruitfulness in your life is found in one word of eternal significance: "Yes." Your commission is clear: As a king and priest cleansed by the blood of Jesus, your lifelong calling is to offer the fire and incense of prayer, praise, worship, and intercession to the Most High God and to intercede on behalf of this lost and dying generation.

Allow the Spirit of Pentecost to fall on you again in all of His fire and glory. Find those of like mind who also have discovered the secrets and power of God's altar of prayer. Join with one or two others to harmonize your requests to God as you restore the Watch of the Lord in your area. Work with your pastor or church members to raise up a "house of prayer for all nations" that truly fulfills the desire of God.

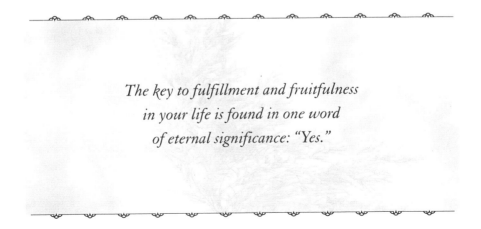

*The key to fulfillment and fruitfulness
in your life is found in one word
of eternal significance: "Yes."*

Pray for the harvest, for workers of the harvest. Seek the face of Him who bared His right arm in Christ Jesus and redeemed you from the kingdom of darkness. Then, do anything and everything that He tells you to do with all of your heart. The Moravians discovered the secret place of power called prayer. They also lived out another secret of effective Christian living—that *all men and women* are ministers of the gospel of Jesus and stewards of a sacred hope that must be trumpeted to hurting people at every occasion. It is time to mount the Watch of the Lord. It is time to light the watch fires and restore the lost art of intercession, the ancient tool of the Lord, to the Church of the Lord. Let it begin!

A Prayer of Consecration

Here I am, Lord. Possess me with your Holy Life. Teach me to release the highest weapon of spiritual warfare—the brillance of your great Presence. Let the fire of your hot love burn on the altar of my heart. Let there be fire on my altar and may it never go out. Count me in. Sign me up as a watchman on your wall. Restore the lost art of intercession. Restore the power and the passion of the watch of the Lord. Use me in Your End Time Army and set me as an intercessor for Christ's namesake. Amen.

Endnotes

1. Rev. John Greenfield, *Power From on High or the Two Hundredth Anniversary of the Great Moravian Revival, 1727-1927* (Atlantic City, NJ: The World Wide Revival Prayer Movement, 1927), 23.

2. Greenfield, *Power*, 13-14.

3. Greenfield, *Power*, 16-17.

4. Greenfield, *Power*, 54-55.

5. Greenfield, *Power*, 23.

6. Greenfield, *Power*, 19.

7. Greenfield, *Power*, 67.

BOOK TWO

POWER THROUGH PRAYER

E. M. BOUNDS

About the Author

Edward McKendree Bounds (1835-1913), Methodist minister and devotional writer, was born in Shelby County, Missouri. He studied law and was admitted to the bar at age 21. After practicing law for three years, he began preaching for the Methodist Episcopal Church, South. At the time of his pastorate at Brunswick, Missouri, war was declared, and he was made a prisoner of war for refusing to take the oath of allegiance to the federal government. After his release he served as chaplain of the Fifth Missouri regiment (for the Confederate Army) until the close of the war, when he was captured and held as a prisoner in Nashville, Tennessee. After the war ended, Bounds served as pastor of churches in Tennessee, Alabama, and St. Louis, Missouri. Bounds spent the last 17 years of his life with his family in Washington, Georgia, writing his "Spiritual Life Books."

CHAPTER 1

Men of Prayer Needed

We are constantly on a stretch, if not on a strain, to devise new methods, new plans, new organizations to advance the Church and secure enlargement and efficiency for the gospel. This trend of the day has a tendency to lose sight of the man or sink the man in the plan or organization. God's plan is to make much of the man, far more of him than of anything else. Men are God's method. *The Church is looking for better methods; God is looking for better men.*

"There was a man sent from God whose name was John." The dispensation that heralded and prepared the way for Christ was bound up in that man John. "Unto us a child is born, unto us a son is given." The world's salvation comes out of that cradled Son. When Paul appeals to the personal character of the men who rooted the gospel in the world, he solves the mystery of their success. The glory and efficiency of the gospel is staked on the men who proclaim it. When God declares that "the eyes of the Lord run to and fro throughout the whole earth, to show Himself strong in the behalf of them whose heart is perfect toward him," He declares the necessity of men and His dependence on them as a channel through which to exert His power upon the world. This vital, urgent truth is one that this age of machinery is apt to forget. The forgetting of it is as baneful on the work of God as would be the striking of the sun from its sphere. Darkness, confusion, and death would ensue.

What the Church needs today is not more machinery or better, not new organizations or more and novel methods, but men whom the Holy Ghost can use—men of prayer, men mighty in prayer. The Holy Ghost does not flow through methods, but through men. He does not come on machinery, but on men. He does not anoint plans, but men—men of prayer.

An eminent historian has said that the accidents of personal character have more to do with the revolutions of nations than either philosophic historians or democratic politicians will allow. This truth has its application in full to the gospel of Christ, the character and conduct of the followers of Christ—Christianize the world, transfigure nations and individuals. Of the preachers of the gospel it is eminently true.

The character as well as the fortunes of the gospel is committed to the preacher. He makes or mars the message from God to man. The preacher is the golden pipe through which the divine oil flows. The pipe must not only be golden, but open and flawless, that the oil may have a full, unhindered, unwasted flow.

The man makes the preacher. God must make the man. The messenger is, if possible, more than the message. The preacher is more than the sermon. The preacher makes the sermon. As the life-giving milk from the mother's bosom is but the mother's life, so all the preacher says is tinctured, impregnated by what the preacher is. The treasure is in earthen vessels, and the taste of the vessel impregnates and may discolor. The man, the whole man, lies behind the sermon. Preaching is not the performance of an hour. It is the outflow of a life. It takes 20 years to make a sermon, because it takes 20 years to make the man. The true sermon is a thing of life. The sermon grows because the man grows. The sermon is forceful because the man is forceful. The sermon is holy because the man is holy. The sermon is full of the divine unction because the man is full of the divine unction.

Paul termed it "my gospel"; not that he had degraded it by his personal eccentricities or diverted it by selfish appropriation, but the gospel was put into the heart and lifeblood of the man Paul, as a personal trust to be executed by his Pauline traits, to be set aflame and empowered by the fiery energy of his fiery soul. Paul's sermons—what were they? Where are they? Skeletons, scattered fragments, afloat on the sea of inspiration! But the man Paul, greater than his sermons, lives forever, in full form, feature, and stature, with his molding hand on the Church. The preaching is but a voice. The voice in silence dies, the text is forgotten, the sermon fades from memory; the preacher lives.

The sermon cannot rise in its life-giving forces above the man. Dead men give out dead sermons, and dead sermons kill. Everything depends on the spiritual character of the preacher. Under the Jewish dispensation the high priest had inscribed in jeweled letters on a golden frontlet: "Holiness to the Lord." So every preacher in Christ's ministry must be molded into and mastered by this same holy motto. It is a crying shame for the Christian ministry to fall lower in holiness of character and holiness of aim than the Jewish priesthood. Jonathan Edwards said: "I went on with my eager pursuit after more holiness and conformity to Christ. The heaven I desired was a heaven of holiness."

The gospel of Christ does not move by popular waves. It has no self-propagating power. It moves as the men who have charge of it move. The preacher must impersonate the gospel. Its divine, most distinctive features must be embodied in him. The constraining power of love must be in the preacher as a projecting, eccentric, all-commanding, self-oblivious force. The energy of self-denial must be his being, his heart and blood and bones. He must go forth as a man among men, clothed with humility, abiding in meekness, wise as a serpent, harmless as a dove; the bonds of a servant with the spirit of a king, a king in high, royal, independent bearing, with the simplicity and sweetness of a child. The preacher must throw himself, with all the abandon of a perfect, self-emptying faith and a self-consuming zeal, into his work for the salvation of men.

Hearty, heroic, compassionate, fearless martyrs must the men be who take hold of and shape a generation for God. If they be timid time servers, place seekers, if they be men pleasers or men fearers, if their faith has a weak hold on God or His Word, if their denial be broken by any phase of self or the world, they cannot take hold of the Church nor the world for God.

The preacher's sharpest and strongest preaching should be to himself. His most difficult, delicate, laborious, and thorough work must be with himself. The training of the 12 disciples was the great, difficult, and enduring work of Christ. Preachers are not sermon makers, but men makers and saint makers, and he only is well-trained for this business who has made himself a man and a saint. It is not great talents nor great learning nor great preachers that God needs, but men great in holiness, great in faith, great in love, great in fidelity, great for God—men always preaching by holy sermons in the pulpit, by holy lives out of it. These can mold a generation for God.

After this order, the early Christians were formed. Men they were of solid mold, preachers after the heavenly type—heroic, stalwart, soldierly, saintly. Preaching with them meant self-denying, self-crucifying, serious, toilsome, martyr business. They applied themselves to it in a way that told on their generation, and formed in its womb a generation yet unborn for God. The preaching man is to be the praying man. Prayer is the preacher's mightiest weapon. An almighty force in itself, it gives life and force to all.

The real sermon is made in the closet. The man—God's man—is made in the closet. His life and his profoundest convictions were born in his secret communion with God. The burdened and tearful agony of his spirit, his weightiest and sweetest messages were got when alone with God. Prayer makes the man; prayer makes the preacher; prayer makes the pastor.

The pulpit of this day is weak in praying. The pride of learning is against the dependent humility of prayer. Prayer is with the pulpit too often only official—a performance for the routine of service. Prayer is not to the modern pulpit the mighty force it was in Paul's life or Paul's ministry. Every preacher who does not make prayer a mighty factor in his own life and ministry is weak as a factor in God's work and is powerless to project God's cause in this world.

CHAPTER 2

Our Sufficiency Is of God

The sweetest graces by a slight perversion may bear the bitterest fruit. The sun gives life, but sunstrokes are death. Preaching is to give life; it may kill. The preacher holds the keys; he may lock as well as unlock. Preaching is God's great institution for the planting and maturing of spiritual life. When properly executed, its benefits are untold; when wrongly executed, no evil can exceed its damaging results. It is an easy matter to destroy the flock if the shepherd be unwary or the pasture be destroyed, easy to capture the citadel if the watchmen be asleep or the food and water be poisoned. Invested with such gracious prerogatives, exposed to so great evils, involving so many grave responsibilities, it would be a parody on the shrewdness of the devil and a libel on his character and reputation if he did not bring his master influences to adulterate the preacher and the preaching. In face of all this, the exclamatory interrogatory of Paul, "Who is sufficient for these things?" is never out of order.

Paul says: "Our sufficiency is of God, who also hath made us able ministers of the new testament; not of the letter, but of the spirit: for the letter killeth, but the spirit giveth life." The true ministry is God-touched, God-enabled, and

God-made. The Spirit of God is on the preacher in anointing power, the fruit of the Spirit is in his heart, the Spirit of God has vitalized the man and the word; his preaching gives life, gives life as the spring gives life; gives life as the resurrection gives life; gives ardent life as the summer gives ardent life; gives fruitful life as the autumn gives fruitful life. The life-giving preacher is a man of God, whose heart is ever athirst for God, whose soul is ever following hard after God, whose eye is single to God, and in whom by the power of God's Spirit the flesh and the world have been crucified and his ministry is like the generous flood of a life-giving river.

The preaching that kills is non-spiritual preaching. The ability of the preaching is not from God. Lower sources than God have given to it energy and stimulant. The Spirit is not evident in the preacher nor his preaching. Many kinds of forces may be projected and stimulated by preaching that kills, but they are not spiritual forces. They may resemble spiritual forces, but are only the shadow, the counterfeit; life they may seem to have, but the life is magnetized. The preaching that kills is the letter; shapely and orderly it may be, but it is the letter still, the dry, husky letter, the empty, bald shell. The letter may have the germ of life in it, but it has no breath of spring to evoke it; winter seeds they are, as hard as the winter's soil, as icy as the winter's air, no thawing nor germinating by them.

This letter-preaching has the truth. But even divine truth has no life-giving energy alone; it must be energized by the Spirit, with all God's forces at its back. Truth unquickened by God's Spirit deadens as much as, or more than, error. It may be the truth without admixture; but without the Spirit its shade and touch are deadly, its truth error, its light darkness. The letter-preaching is unctionless, neither mellowed nor oiled by the Spirit. There may be tears, but tears cannot run God's machinery; tears may be but summer's breath on a snow-covered iceberg, nothing but surface slush. Feelings and earnestness there may be, but it is the emotion of the actor and the earnestness of the attorney. The preacher may feel from the kindling of his own sparks, be eloquent over his own exegesis, earnest in delivering the product of his own brain; the professor may usurp the place and imitate the fire of the apostle; brains and nerves may serve the place and feign the work of God's Spirit, and by these forces the letter may glow and sparkle like an illumined text, but the glow and sparkle will be as barren of life as the field sown with pearls.

The death-dealing element lies back of the words, back of the sermon, back of the occasion, back of the manner, back of the action. The great hindrance is in the preacher himself. He has not in himself the mighty life-creating forces. There may be no discount on his orthodoxy, honesty, cleanness, or earnestness; but somehow the man, the inner man, in its secret places has never broken down and surrendered to God, his inner life is not a great highway for the transmission of God's message, God's power. Somehow self and not God rules in the holy of holiest. Somewhere, all unconscious to himself, some spiritual nonconductor has touched his inner being, and the divine current has been arrested. His inner being has never felt its thorough spiritual bankruptcy, its utter powerlessness; he has never learned to cry out with an ineffable cry of self-despair and self-helplessness till God's power and God's fire comes in and fills, purifies, empowers.

Self-esteem, self-ability in some pernicious shape has defamed and violated the temple that should be held sacred for God. Life-giving preaching costs the preacher much—death to self, crucifixion to the world, the travail of his own soul. Crucified preaching only can give life. Crucified preaching can come only from a crucified man.

CHAPTER 3

The Letter Killeth

The preaching that kills may be, and often is, orthodox—dogmatically, inviolably orthodox. We love orthodoxy. It is good. It is the best. It is the clean, clear-cut teaching of God's Word, the trophies won by truth in its conflict with error, the levees that faith has raised against the desolating floods of honest or reckless misbelief or unbelief; but orthodoxy, clear and hard as crystal, suspicious and militant, may be but the letter well-shaped, well-named, and well-learned, the letter which kills. Nothing is so dead as a dead orthodoxy, too dead to speculate, too dead to think, to study, or to pray.

The preaching that kills may have insight and grasp of principles, may be scholarly and critical in taste, may have every minutia of the derivation and grammar of the letter, may be able to trim the letter into its perfect pattern, and illume it as Plato and Cicero may be illumined, may study it as a lawyer studies his textbooks to form his brief or to defend his case, and yet be like a frost, a killing frost. Letter-preaching may be eloquent, enameled with poetry and rhetoric, sprinkled with prayer spiced with sensation, illumined by genius and yet these be but the massive or chaste, costly mountings, the rare and beautiful flowers which coffin the corpse. The preaching that kills may be without scholarship, unmarked by any freshness of thought or feeling, clothed in tasteless generalities or vapid specialties, with style irregular, slovenly, savoring neither of closet nor of study, graced neither by thought, expression, or prayer. Under such preaching how wide and utter the desolation! How profound the spiritual death!

This letter-preaching deals with the surface and shadow of things, and not the things themselves. It does not penetrate the inner part. It has no deep insight into, no strong grasp of, the hidden life of God's Word. It is true to the outside, but the outside is the hull that must be broken and penetrated for the kernel. The letter may be dressed so as to attract and be fashionable, but the attraction is not toward God nor is the fashion for Heaven.

The failure is in the preacher. God has not made him. He has never been in the hands of God like clay in the hands of the potter. He has been busy about the sermon, its thought and finish, its drawing and impressive forces; but the deep things of God have never been sought, studied, fathomed, experienced by him. He has never stood before "the throne high and lifted up," never heard the seraphim song, never seen the vision nor felt the rush of that awful holiness, and cried out in utter abandon and despair under the sense of weakness and guilt, and had his life renewed, his heart touched, purged, inflamed by the live coal from God's altar. His ministry may draw people to him, to the Church, to the form and ceremony; but no true drawings to God, no sweet, holy, divine communion induced. The Church has been frescoed but not edified, pleased but not sanctified. Life is suppressed; a chill is on the summer air; the soil is baked. The city of our God becomes the city of the dead; the Church a graveyard, not an embattled army. Praise and prayer are stifled; worship is dead. The preacher and the preaching have helped sin, not holiness; peopled hell, not Heaven.

Preaching that kills is prayerless preaching. Without prayer the preacher creates death, and not life. The preacher who is feeble in prayer is feeble in life-giving forces. The preacher who has retired prayer as a conspicuous and largely prevailing element in his own character has shorn his preaching of its distinctive life-giving power. Professional praying there is and will be, but professional praying helps the preaching to its deadly work. Professional praying chills and kills both preaching and praying.

Much of the lax devotion and lazy, irreverent attitudes in congregational praying are attributable to professional praying in the pulpit. Long, discursive, dry, and inane are the prayers in many pulpits. Without unction or heart, they fall like a killing frost on all the graces of worship. Death-dealing prayers they are. Every vestige of devotion has perished under their breath. The deader they are the longer they grow. A plea for short praying, live praying, real heart praying, praying by the Holy Spirit—direct, specific, ardent, simple, unctuous in the pulpit—is in order. A school to teach preachers how to pray, as God counts praying, would be more beneficial to true piety, true worship, and true preaching than all theological schools.

Stop! Pause! Consider! Where are we? What are we doing? Preaching to kill? Praying to kill? Praying to God! The great God, the Maker of all worlds, the Judge of all men! What reverence! What simplicity! What sincerity! What truth in the inward parts is demanded! How real we must be! How hearty! Prayer to God the noblest exercise, the loftiest effort of man, the most real thing! Shall we not discard forever accursed preaching that kills and prayer that kills, and do the real thing, the mightiest thing— prayerful praying, life-creating preaching, bring the mightiest force to bear on Heaven and earth and draw on God's exhaustless and open treasure for the need and beggary of man?

CHAPTER 4

Tendencies to Be Avoided

There are two extreme tendencies in the ministry. The one is to shut it-self out from intercourse with the people. The monk, the hermit were illus-trations of this; they shut themselves out from men to be more with God. They failed, of course. Our being with God is of use only as we expend its priceless benefits on men. This age, neither with preacher nor with people, is much intent on God. Our hankering is not that way. We shut ourselves to our study, we become students, bookworms, Bible worms, sermon makers, noted for literature, thought, and sermons; but the people and God, where are they? Out of heart, out of mind. Preachers who are great thinkers, great students, must be the greatest of prayers, or else they will be the greatest of backsliders, heartless professionals, rationalistic, less than the least of preachers in God's estimate.

The other tendency is to thoroughly popularize the ministry. He is no longer God's man, but a man of affairs, of the people. He prays not, because his mission is to the people. If he can move the people, create an interest, a sen-sation in favor of religion, an interest in Church work—he is satisfied. His personal relation to God is no factor in his work. Prayer has little or no place in his plans. The disaster and ruin of such a ministry cannot be computed by earthly arithmetic. What the preacher is in prayer to God, for himself, for his people, so is his power for real good to men, so is his true fruitfulness, his true fidelity to God, to man, for time, for eternity.

It is impossible for the preacher to keep his spirit in harmony with the divine nature of his high calling without much prayer. That the preacher by dint of duty and laborious fidelity to the work and routine of the ministry can keep himself in trim and fitness is a serious mistake. Even sermon-making, incessant and taxing as an art, as a duty, as a work, or as a pleasure, will engross and harden, will estrange the heart, by neglect of prayer, from God. The scientist loses God in nature. The preacher may lose God in his sermon.

Prayer freshens the heart of the preacher, keeps it in tune with God and in sympathy with the people, lifts his ministry out of the chilly air of a profession, fructifies routine and moves every wheel with the facility and power of a divine unction.

Mr. Spurgeon says: "Of course the preacher is above all others distinguished as a man of prayer. He prays as an ordinary Christian, else he were a hypocrite. He prays more than ordinary Christians, else he were disqualified for the office he has undertaken. If you as ministers are not very prayerful, you are to be pitied. If you become lax in sacred devotion, not only will you need to be pitied but your people also, and the day cometh in which you shall be ashamed and confounded. All our libraries and studies are mere emptiness compared with our closets. Our seasons of fasting and prayer at the Tabernacle have been high days indeed; never has Heaven's gate stood wider; never have our hearts been nearer the central Glory."

The praying that makes a prayerful ministry is not a little praying put in as we put flavor to give it a pleasant smack, but the praying must be in the body, and form the blood and bones. Prayer is no petty duty, put into a corner; no piecemeal performance made out of the fragments of time which have been snatched from business and other engagements of life; but it means that the best of our time, the heart of our time and strength must be given. It does not mean the closet absorbed in the study or swallowed up in the activities of ministerial duties; but it means the closet first, the study and activities second, both study and activities freshened and made efficient by the closet. Prayer that affects one's ministry must give tone to one's life. The praying that gives color and bent to character is no pleasant, hurried pastime. It must enter as strongly into the heart and life as Christ's "strong crying and tears" did; must draw out the soul into an agony of desire as Paul's did; must be an inwrought fire and force like the "effectual, fervent prayer" of James; must be of that quality which, when put into the golden censer and incensed before God, works mighty spiritual throes and revolutions.

Prayer is not a little habit pinned onto us while we were tied to our mother's apron strings; neither is it a little decent quarter of a minute's grace said over an hour's dinner, but it is a most serious work of our most serious years. It engages more of time and appetite than our longest dinings or richest feasts. The prayer that makes much of our preaching must be made much of. The character of our praying will determine the character of our preaching. Light praying will make light preaching. Prayer makes preaching strong, gives it unction, and makes it stick. In every ministry weighty for good, prayer has always been a serious business.

The preacher must be preeminently a man of prayer. His heart must graduate in the school of prayer. In the school of prayer only can the heart learn to preach. No learning can make up for the failure to pray. No earnestness, no diligence, no study, no gifts will supply its lack.

Talking to men for God is a great thing, but talking to God for men is greater still. *He will never talk well and with real success to men for God who has not learned well how to talk to God for men.* More than this, prayerless words in the pulpit and out of it are deadening words.

CHAPTER 5

Prayer, the Great Essential

Prayer, in the preacher's life, in the preacher's study, in the preacher's pulpit, must be a conspicuous and an all-impregnating force and an all-coloring ingredient. It must play no secondary part, be no mere coating. To him it is given to be with his Lord "all night in prayer." The preacher, to train himself in self-denying prayer, is charged to look to his Master, who, "rising up a great while before day, went out, and departed into a solitary place, and there prayed." The preacher's study ought to be a closet, a Bethel, an altar, a vision, and a ladder, that every thought might ascend heavenward ere it went manward; that every part of the sermon might be scented by the air of Heaven and made serious, because God was in the study.

As the engine never moves until the fire is kindled, so preaching, with all its machinery, perfection, and polish, is at a dead standstill, as far as spiritual results are concerned, till prayer has kindled and created the steam. The texture, fineness, and strength of the sermon is as so much rubbish unless the mighty impulse of prayer is in it, through it, and behind it. The preacher must, by prayer, put God in the sermon. The preacher must, by prayer, move God toward the people before he can move the people to God by his words.

The preacher must have had audience and ready access to God before he can have access to the people. An open way to God for the preacher is the surest pledge of an open way to the people.

It is necessary to iterate and reiterate that prayer, as a mere habit, as a performance gone through by routine or in a professional way, is a dead and rotten thing. Such praying has no connection with the praying for which we plead. We are stressing true praying, which engages and sets on fire every high element of the preacher's being—prayer that is born of vital oneness with Christ and the fullness of the Holy Ghost, which springs from the deep, overflowing fountains of tender compassion, deathless solicitude for man's eternal good; a consuming zeal for the glory of God; a thorough conviction of the preacher's difficult and delicate work and of the imperative need of God's mightiest help. Praying grounded on these solemn and profound convictions is the only true praying. Preaching backed by such praying is the only preaching that sows the seeds of eternal life in human hearts and builds men up for Heaven.

It is true that there may be popular preaching, pleasant preaching, taking preaching, preaching of much intellectual, literary, and brainy force, with its measure and form of good, with little or no praying; but the preaching that secures God's end in preaching must be born of prayer from text to exordium, delivered with the energy and spirit of prayer, followed and made to germinate, and kept in vital force in the hearts of the hearers by the preacher's prayers, long after the occasion has past.

We may excuse the spiritual poverty of our preaching in many ways, but the true secret will be found in the lack of urgent prayer for God's presence in the power of the Holy Spirit. There are preachers innumerable who can deliver masterful sermons after their order; but the effects are short-lived and do not enter as a factor at all into the regions of the spirit where the fearful war between God and satan, Heaven and hell, is being waged because they are not made powerfully militant and spiritually victorious by prayer.

The preachers who gain mighty results for God are the men who have prevailed in their pleadings with God ere venturing to plead with men. The preachers who are the mightiest in their closets with God are the mightiest in their pulpits with men.

Preachers are human folks, and are exposed to and often caught by the strong driftings of human currents. Praying is spiritual work; and human nature does not like taxing, spiritual work. Human nature wants to sail to Heaven under a favoring breeze, a full, smooth sea. Prayer is humbling work. It abases intellect and pride, crucifies vainglory, and signs our spiritual bankruptcy, and all these are hard for flesh and blood to bear. It is easier not to pray than to bear them. So we come to one of the crying evils of these times, maybe of all times—little or no praying. Of these two evils, perhaps little praying is worse than no praying. Little praying is a kind of make-believe, a salvo for the conscience, a farce and a delusion.

The little estimate we put on prayer is evident from the little time we give to it. The time given to prayer by the average preacher scarcely counts in the sum of the daily aggregate. Not infrequently the preacher's only praying is by his bedside in his nightdress, ready for bed and soon in it, with, perchance the addition of a few hasty snatches of prayer ere he is dressed in the morning. How feeble, vain, and little is such praying compared with the time and energy devoted to praying by holy men in and out of the Bible! How poor and mean our petty, childish praying is beside the habits of the true men of God in all ages! To men who think praying their main business and devote time to it according to this high estimate of its importance does God commit the keys of His Kingdom, and by them does He work His spiritual wonders in this world. Great praying is the sign and seal of God's great leaders and the earnest of the conquering forces with which God will crown their labors.

The preacher is commissioned to pray as well as to preach. His mission is incomplete if he does not do both well. The preacher may speak with all the eloquence of men and of angels; but unless he can pray with a faith that draws all Heaven to his aid, his preaching will be "as sounding brass or a tinkling cymbal" for permanent God-honoring, soul-saving uses.

CHAPTER 6

A Praying Ministry Successful

It may be put down as a spiritual axiom that in every truly successful ministry prayer is an evident and controlling force—evident and controlling in the life of the preacher, evident and controlling in the deep spirituality of his work. A ministry may be a very thoughtful ministry without prayer; the preacher may secure fame and popularity without prayer; the whole machinery of the preacher's life and work may be run without the oil of prayer or with scarcely enough to grease one cog; but no ministry can be a spiritual one, securing holiness in the preacher and in his people, without prayer being made an evident and controlling force.

The preacher who prays indeed puts God into the work. God does not come into the preacher's work as a matter of course or on general principles, but He comes by prayer and special urgency. That God will be found of us in the day that we seek Him with the whole heart is as true of the preacher as of the penitent. A prayerful ministry is the only ministry that brings the preacher into sympathy with the people. Prayer as essentially unites to the human as it does to the divine. A prayerful ministry is the only ministry qualified for the high offices and responsibilities of the preacher. Colleges, learning, books, theology, preaching cannot make a preacher, but praying does. The apostles' commission to preach was a blank till filled up by the Pentecost that praying brought.

A prayerful minister has passed beyond the regions of the popular, beyond the man of mere affairs, of secularities, of pulpit attractiveness; passed beyond the ecclesiastical organizer or general into a sublimer and mightier region, the region of the spiritual. Holiness is the product of his work; transfigured hearts and lives emblazon the reality of his work, its trueness and substantial nature. God is with him. His ministry is not projected on worldly or surface principles. He is deeply stored with and deeply schooled in the things of God. His long, deep communings with God about his people and the agony of his wrestling spirit have crowned him as a prince in the things of God. The iciness of the mere professional has long since melted under the intensity of his praying.

The superficial results of many a ministry, the deadness of others, are to be found in the lack of praying. No ministry can succeed without much praying, and this praying must be fundamental, ever-abiding, ever-increasing. The text, the sermon, should be the result of prayer. The study should be bathed in prayer, all its duties so impregnated with prayer, its whole spirit the spirit of prayer. "I am sorry that I have prayed so little," was the deathbed regret of one of God's chosen ones, a sad and remorseful regret for a preacher. "I want a life of greater, deeper, truer prayer," said the late Archbishop Tait. So may we all say, and this may we all secure.

God's true preachers have been distinguished by one great feature: they were men of prayer. Differing often in many things, they have always had a common center. They may have started from different points, and traveled by different roads, but they converged to one point: they were one in prayer. God to them was the center of attraction, and prayer was the path that led to God. These men prayed not occasionally, not a little at regular or at odd times; but they so prayed that their prayers entered into and shaped their characters; they so prayed as to affect their own lives and the lives of others; they so prayed as to make the history of the Church and influence the current of the times. They spent much time in prayer, not because they marked the shadow on the dial or the hands on the clock, but because it was to them so momentous and engaging a business that they could scarcely give over.

Prayer was to them what it was to Paul, a striving with earnest effort of soul; what it was to Jacob, a wrestling and prevailing; what it was to Christ, "strong crying and tears." They "prayed always with all prayer and supplication in the Spirit, and watching thereunto with all perseverance." "The effectual, fervent prayer" has been the mightiest weapon of God's mightiest soldiers. The statement in regard to Elijah—that he "was a man subject to like passions as we are, and he prayed earnestly that it might not rain: and it rained not on the earth by the space of three years and six months. And he prayed again, and the heaven gave rain, and the earth brought forth her fruit"—comprehends all prophets and preachers who have moved their generation for God, and shows the instrument by which they worked their wonders.

CHAPTER 7

Much Time Should Be Given to Prayer

While many private prayers, in the nature of things, must be short; while public prayers, as a rule, ought to be short and condensed; while there is ample room for and value put on ejaculatory prayer—yet in our private communions with God time is a feature essential to its value. Much time spent with God is the secret of all successful praying. Prayer that is felt as a mighty force is the mediate or immediate product of much time spent with God. Our short prayers owe their point and efficiency to the long ones that have preceded them. The short prevailing prayer cannot be prayed by one who has not prevailed with God in a mightier struggle of long continuance.

Jacob's victory of faith could not have been gained without that all-night wrestling. God's acquaintance is not made by pop calls. God does not bestow His gifts on the casual or hasty comers and goers. Much with God alone is the secret of knowing Him and of influence with Him. He yields to the persistency of a faith that knows Him. He bestows His richest gifts upon those who declare their desire for and appreciation of those gifts by the constancy as well as earnestness of their importunity.

Christ, who in this as well as other things is our Example, spent many whole nights in prayer. His custom was to pray much. He had His habitual place to pray. Many long seasons of praying make up His history and character. Paul prayed day and night. It took time from very important interests for Daniel to pray three times a day. David's morning, noon, and night praying were doubtless on many occasions very protracted. While we have no specific account of the time these Bible saints spent in prayer, yet the indications are that they consumed much time in prayer, and on some occasions long seasons of praying was their custom.

We would not have any think that the value of their prayers is to be measured by the clock, but our purpose is to impress on our minds the necessity of being much alone with God; and that if this feature has not been produced by our faith, then our faith is of a feeble and surface type.

The men who have most fully illustrated Christ in their character, and have most powerfully affected the world for Him, have been men who spent so much time with God as to make it a notable feature of their lives. Charles Simeon devoted the hours from four till eight in the morning to God. Mr. Wesley spent two hours daily in prayer. He began at four in the morning. Of him, one who knew him well wrote: "He thought prayer to be more his business than anything else, and I have seen him come out of his closet with a serenity of face next to shining." John Fletcher stained the walls of his room by the breath of his prayers. Sometimes he would pray all night; always, frequently, and with great earnestness. His whole life was a life of prayer. "I would not rise from my seat," he said, "without lifting my heart to God." His greeting to a friend was always: "Do I meet you praying?" Luther said: "If I fail to spend two hours in prayer each morning, the devil gets the victory through the day. I have so much business I cannot get on without spending three hours daily in prayer." He had a motto: "He that has prayed well has studied well."

Archbishop Leighton was so much alone with God that he seemed to be in a perpetual meditation. "Prayer and praise were his business and his pleasure," says his biographer. Bishop Ken was so much with God that his soul was said to be God-enamored. He was with God before the clock struck three every morning. Bishop Asbury said: "I propose to rise at four o'clock as often as I can and spend two hours in prayer and meditation." Samuel Rutherford, the fragrance of whose piety is still rich, rose at three in the morning to meet God in prayer. Joseph Alleine arose at four o'clock for his business of praying till eight. If he heard other tradesmen plying their business before he was up, he would exclaim: "O how this shames me! Doth not my Master deserve more than theirs?" He who has learned this trade well draws at will, on sight, and with acceptance of Heaven's unfailing bank.

One of the holiest and among the most gifted of Scotch preachers says: "I ought to spend the best hours in communion with God. It is my noblest and most fruitful employment, and is not to be thrust into a corner. The morning hours, from six to eight, are the most uninterrupted and should be thus employed. After tea is my best hour, and that should be solemnly dedicated to God. I ought not to give up the good old habit of prayer before going to bed; but guard must be kept against sleep. When I awake in the night, I ought to rise and pray. A little time after breakfast might be given to intercession." This was the praying plan of Robert McCheyne. The memorable Methodist band in their praying shame us. "From four to five in the morning, private prayer; from five to six in the evening, private prayer."

John Welch, the holy and wonderful Scotch preacher, thought the day ill spent if he did not spend eight or ten hours in prayer. He kept a plaid that he might wrap himself when he arose to pray at night. His wife would complain when she found him lying on the ground weeping. He would reply: "O woman, I have the souls of three thousand to answer for, and I know not how it is with many of them!"

CHAPTER 8

Examples of Praying Men

Bishop Wilson says: "In H. Martyn's journal the spirit of prayer, the time he devoted to the duty, and his fervor in it are the first things which strike me."

Payson wore the hardwood boards into grooves where his knees pressed so often and so long. His biographer says: "His continuing instant in prayer, be his circumstances what they might, is the most noticeable fact in his history, and points out the duty of all who would rival his eminency. To his ardent and persevering prayers must no doubt be ascribed in a great measure his distinguished and almost uninterrupted success."

The Marquis DeRenty, to whom Christ was most precious, ordered his servant to call him from his devotions at the end of half an hour. The servant at the time saw his face through an aperture. It was marked with such holiness that he hated to arouse him. His lips were moving, but he was perfectly silent. He waited until three half hours had passed; then he called to him, when he arose from his knees, saying that the half hour was so short when he was communing with Christ.

Brainerd said: "I love to be alone in my cottage, where I can spend much time in prayer."

William Bramwell is famous in Methodist annals for personal holiness and for his wonderful success in preaching and for the marvelous answers to his prayers. For hours at a time he would pray. He almost lived on his knees. He went over his circuits like a flame of fire. The fire was kindled by the time he spent in prayer. He often spent as much as four hours in a single season of prayer in retirement.

Bishop Andrewes spent the greatest part of five hours every day in prayer and devotion.

Sir Henry Havelock always spent the first two hours of each day alone with God. If the encampment was struck at 6 A.M., he would rise at four.

Earl Cairns rose daily at six o'clock to secure an hour and a half for the study of the Bible and for prayer, before conducting family worship at a quarter to eight.

Dr. Judson's success in prayer is attributable to the fact that he gave much time to prayer. He says on this point:

> Arrange thy affairs, if possible, so that thou canst leisurely devote two or three hours every day not merely to devotional exercises but to the very act of secret prayer and communion with God. Endeavor seven times a day to withdraw from business and company and lift up thy soul to God in private retirement. Begin the day by rising after midnight and devoting some time amid the silence and darkness of the night to this sacred work. Let the hour of opening dawn find thee at the same work. Let the hours of nine, twelve, three, six, and nine at night witness the same. Be resolute in his cause. Make all practicable sacrifices to maintain it. Consider that thy time is short, and that business and company must not be allowed to rob thee of thy God.

Impossible, say we, fanatical directions! Dr. Judson impressed an empire for Christ and laid the foundations of God's Kingdom with imperishable granite in the heart of Burmah. He was successful, one of the few men who mightily impressed the world for Christ. Many men of greater gifts and genius and learning than he have made no such impression; their religious work is like footsteps in the sands, but he has engraven his work on the adamant. The secret of its profundity and endurance is found in the fact that he gave time to prayer. He kept the iron red-hot with prayer, and God's skill fashioned it with enduring power. No man can do a great and enduring work for God who is not a man of prayer, and no man can be a man of prayer who does not give much time to praying.

Is it true that prayer is simply the compliance with habit, dull and mechanical? A petty performance into which we are trained till tameness, shortness, superficiality are its chief elements? "Is it true that prayer is, as is assumed, little else than the half-passive play of sentiment which flows languidly on through the minutes or hours of easy reverie?" Canon Liddon continues: "Let those who have really prayed give the answer. They sometimes describe prayer with the patriarch Jacob as a wrestling together with an Unseen Power which may last, not unfrequently in an earnest life, late into the night hours, or even to the break of day. Sometimes they refer to common intercession with St. Paul as a concerted struggle. They have, when praying, their eyes fixed on the Great Intercessor in Gethsemane, upon the drops of blood that fall to the ground in that agony of resignation and sacrifice. Importunity is of the essence of successful prayer. Importunity means not dreaminess but sustained work. It is through prayer especially that the kingdom of Heaven suffereth violence and the violent take it by force." It was a saying of the late Bishop Hamilton that "No man is likely to do much good in prayer who does not begin by looking upon it in the light of a work to be prepared for and persevered in with all the earnestness which we bring to bear upon subjects which are in our opinion at once most interesting and most necessary."

CHAPTER 9

Begin the Day With Prayer

The men who have done the most for God in this world have been early on their knees. He who fritters away the early morning, its opportunity and freshness, in other pursuits than seeking God will make poor headway seeking Him the rest of the day. If God is not first in our thoughts and efforts in the morning, He will be in the last place the remainder of the day.

Behind this early rising and early praying is the ardent desire that presses us into this pursuit after God. Morning listlessness is the index to a listless heart. The heart that is behindhand in seeking God in the morning has lost its relish for God. David's heart was ardent after God. He hungered and thirsted after God, and so he sought God early, before daylight. The bed and sleep could not chain his soul in its eagerness after God. Christ longed for communion with God; and so, rising a great while before day, He would go out into the mountain to pray. The disciples, when fully awake and ashamed of their indulgence, would know where to find Him. We might go through the list of men who have mightily impressed the world for God, and we would find them early after God.

A desire for God that cannot break the chains of sleep is a weak thing and will do but little good for God after it has indulged itself fully. The desire for God that keeps so far behind the devil and the world at the beginning of the day will never catch up.

It is not simply the getting up that puts men to the front and makes them captain generals in God's hosts, but it is the ardent desire that stirs and breaks all self-indulgent chains. But the getting up gives vent, increase, and strength to the desire. If they had lain in bed and indulged themselves, the desire would have been quenched. The desire aroused them and put them on the stretch for God, and this heeding and acting on the call gave their faith its grasp on God and gave to their hearts the sweetest and fullest revelation of God, and this strength of faith and fullness of revelation made them saints by eminence, and the halo of their sainthood has come down to us, and we have entered on the enjoyment of their conquests. But we take our fill in enjoyment, and not in productions. We build their tombs and write their epitaphs, but are careful not to follow their examples.

We need a generation of preachers who seek God and seek Him early, who give the freshness and dew of effort to God, and secure in return the freshness and fullness of His power that He may be as the dew to them, full of gladness and strength, through all the heat and labor of the day. Our laziness after God is our crying sin. The children of this world are far wiser than we. They are at it early and late. We do not seek God with ardor and diligence. No man gets God who does not follow hard after Him, and no soul follows hard after God who is not after Him in early morn.

CHAPTER 10

Prayer and Devotion United

Never was there greater need for saintly men and women; more imperative still is the call for saintly, God-devoted preachers. The world moves with gigantic strides. Satan has his hold and rule on the world, and labors to make all its movements subserve his ends. Religion must do its best work, present its most attractive and perfect models. By every means, modern sainthood must be inspired by the loftiest ideals and by the largest possibilities through the Spirit.

Paul lived on his knees, that the Ephesian Church might measure the heights, breadths, and depths of an unmeasurable saintliness, and "be filled with all the fullness of God." Epaphras laid himself out with the exhaustive toil and strenuous conflict of fervent prayer, that the Colossian Church might "stand perfect and complete in all the will of God." Everywhere, everything in apostolic times was on the stretch that the people of God might each and "all come in the unity of the faith, and of the knowledge of the Son of God, unto a perfect man, unto the measure of the stature of the fullness of Christ." No premium was given to dwarfs; no encouragement to an old babyhood. The babies were to grow; the old, instead of feebleness and

209

infirmities, were to bear fruit in old age, and be fat and flourishing. The divinest thing in religion is holy men and holy women.

No amount of money, genius, or culture can move things for God. Holiness energizing the soul, the whole man aflame with love, with desire for more faith, more prayer, more zeal, more consecration—this is the secret of power. These we need and must have, and men must be the incarnation of this God-inflamed devotedness. God's advance has been stayed, His cause crippled: His name dishonored for their lack. Genius (though the loftiest and most gifted), education (though the most learned and refined), position, dignity, place, honored names, high ecclesiastics cannot move this chariot of our God. It is a fiery one, and fiery forces only can move it. The genius of a Milton fails. The imperial strength of a Leo fails. Brainerd's spirit can move it. Brainerd's spirit was on fire for God, on fire for souls. Nothing earthly, worldly, selfish came in to abate in the least the intensity of this all-impelling and all-consuming force and flame.

Prayer is the creator as well as the channel of devotion. The spirit of devotion is the spirit of prayer. Prayer and devotion are united as soul and body are united, as life and the heart are united. **There is no real prayer without devotion, no devotion without prayer.** The preacher must be surrendered to God in the holiest devotion. He is not a professional man, his ministry is not a profession; it is a divine institution, a divine devotion. He is devoted to God. His aim, aspirations, ambition are for God and to God, and to such prayer is as essential as food is to life.

The preacher, above everything else, must be devoted to God. The preacher's relations to God are the insignia and credentials of his ministry. These must be clear, conclusive, unmistakable. No common, surface type of piety must be his. If he does not excel in grace, he does not excel at all. If he does not preach by life, character, conduct, he does not preach at all. If his piety be light, his preaching may be as soft and as sweet as music, as gifted as Apollo, yet its weight will be a feather's weight, visionary, fleeting as the morning cloud or the early dew.

Devotion to God—there is no substitute for this in the preacher's character and conduct. Devotion to a Church, to opinions, to an organization, to orthodoxy—these are paltry, misleading, and vain when they become the source of inspiration, the animus of a call. God must be the mainspring of the preacher's effort, the fountain and crown of all his toil. The name and honor of Jesus Christ, the advance of His cause, must be all in all. The preacher must have no inspiration but the name of Jesus Christ, no ambition but to have Him glorified, no toil but for Him. Then prayer will be a source of his illuminations, the means of perpetual advance, the gauge of his success. The perpetual aim, the only ambition, the preacher can cherish is to have God with him.

Never did the cause of God need perfect illustrations of the possibilities of prayer more than in this age. No age, no person, will be ensamples of the gospel power except the ages or persons of deep and earnest prayer. A prayerless age will have but scant models of divine power. Prayerless hearts will never rise to these Alpine heights. The age may be a better age than the past, but there is an infinite distance between the betterment of an age by the force of an advancing civilization and its betterment by the increase of holiness and Christlikeness by the energy of prayer.

The Jews were much better when Christ came than in the ages before. It was the golden age of their Pharisaic religion. Their golden religious age crucified Christ. Never more praying, never less praying; never more sacrifices, never less sacrifice; never less idolatry, never more idolatry; never more of temple worship, never less of God worship; never more of lip service, never less of heart service (God worshiped by lips whose hearts and hands crucified God's Son!); never more of churchgoers, never less of saints.

It is prayer-force that makes saints. Holy characters are formed by the power of real praying. The more of true saints, the more of praying; the more of praying, the more of true saints.

CHAPTER 11

An Example of Devotion

God has now, and has had, many of these devoted, prayerful preachers—men in whose lives prayer has been a mighty, controlling, conspicuous force. The world has felt their power, God has felt and honored their power, God's cause has moved mightily and swiftly by their prayers, holiness has shone out in their characters with a divine effulgence.

God found one of the men he was looking for in David Brainerd, whose work and name have gone into history. He was no ordinary man, but was capable of shining in any company, the peer of the wise and gifted ones, eminently suited to fill the most attractive pulpits and to labor among the most refined and the cultured, who were so anxious to secure him for their pastor. President Edwards bears testimony that he was "a young man of distinguished talents, had extraordinary knowledge of men and things, had rare conversational powers, excelled in his knowledge of theology, and was truly, for one so young, an extraordinary divine, and especially in all matters relating to experimental religion. I never knew his equal of his age and standing for clear and accurate notions of the nature and essence of true religion. His manner in prayer was almost inimitable, such as I have very rarely known

213

equaled. His learning was very considerable, and he had extraordinary gifts for the pulpit."

No sublimer story has been recorded in earthly annals than that of David Brainerd; no miracle attests with diviner force the truth of Christianity than the life and work of such a man. Alone in the savage wilds of America, struggling day and night with a mortal disease, unschooled in the care of souls, having access to the Indians for a large portion of time only through the bungling medium of a pagan interpreter, with the Word of God in his heart and in his hand, his soul fired with the divine flame, a place and time to pour out his soul to God in prayer, he fully established the worship of God and secured all its gracious results. The Indians were changed with a great change from the lowest besotments of an ignorant and debased heathenism to pure, devout, intelligent Christians; all vice reformed, the external duties of Christianity at once embraced and acted on; family prayer set up; the Sabbath instituted and religiously observed; the internal graces of religion exhibited with growing sweetness and strength.

The solution of these results is found in David Brainerd himself, not in the conditions or accidents but in the man Brainerd. He was God's man, for God first and last and all the time. God could flow unhindered through him. The omnipotence of grace was neither arrested nor straightened by the conditions of his heart; the whole channel was broadened and cleaned out for God's fullest and most powerful passage, so that God with all His mighty forces could come down on the hopeless, savage wilderness, and transform it into His blooming and fruitful garden; for nothing is too hard for God to do if He can get the right kind of a man to do it with.

Brainerd lived the life of holiness and prayer. His diary is full and monotonous with the record of his seasons of fasting, meditation, and retirement. The time he spent in private prayer amounted to many hours daily. "When I return home," he said, "and give myself to meditation, prayer, and fasting, my soul longs for mortification, self-denial, humility, and divorcement from all things of the world." "I have nothing to do," he said, "with earth but only to labor in it honestly for God. I do not desire to live one minute for anything which earth can afford."

After this high order did he pray:

> Feeling somewhat of the sweetness of communion with God and the constraining force of His love, and how admirably it captivates the soul and makes all the desires and affections to center in God, I set apart this day for secret fasting and prayer, to entreat God to direct and bless me with regard to the great work that I have in view of preaching the gospel, and that the Lord would return to me and show me the light of His countenance. I had little life and power in the forenoon. Near the middle of the afternoon God enabled me to wrestle ardently in intercession for my absent friends, but just at night the Lord visited me marvelously in prayer. I think my soul was never in such agony before. I felt no restraint, for the treasures of divine grace were opened to me. I wrestled for absent friends, for the ingathering of souls, for multitudes of poor souls, and for many that I thought were the children of God, personally, in many distant places. I was in such agony from sun half an hour high till near dark that I was all over wet with sweat, but yet it seemed to me I had done nothing. O, my dear Saviour did sweat blood for poor souls! I longed for more compassion toward them. I felt still in a sweet frame, under a sense of divine love and grace, and went to bed in such a frame, with my heart set on God.

It was prayer that gave to his life and ministry their marvelous power.

The men of mighty prayer are men of spiritual might. Prayers never die. Brainerd's whole life was a life of prayer. By day and by night he prayed. Before preaching and after preaching he prayed. Riding through the interminable solitudes of the forests he prayed. On his bed of straw he prayed. Retiring to the dense and lonely forests, he prayed. Hour by hour, day after day, early morn and late at night, he was praying and fasting, pouring out his soul, interceding, communing with God. He was with God mightily in prayer, and God was with him mightily, and by it he being dead yet speaketh and worketh, and will speak and work till the end comes, and among the glorious ones of that glorious day he will be with the first.

Jonathan Edwards says of him:

> His life shows the right way to success in the works of the ministry. He sought it as the soldier seeks victory in a siege or battle; or as a man that runs a race for a great prize. Animated with love to Christ and souls, how did he labor? Always fervently. Not only in word and doctrine, in public and in private, but in prayers by day and night, wrestling with God in secret and travailing in birth with unutterable groans and agonies, until Christ was formed in the hearts of the people to whom he was sent. Like a true son of Jacob, he persevered in wrestling through all the darkness of the night, until the breaking of the day!

CHAPTER 12

Heart Preparation Necessary

Prayer, with its manifold and many-sided forces, helps the mouth to utter the truth in its fullness and freedom. The preacher is to be prayed for; the preacher is made by prayer. The preacher's mouth is to be prayed for; his mouth is to be opened and filled by prayer. A holy mouth is made by praying, by much praying; a brave mouth is made by praying, by much praying. The Church and the world, God and Heaven, owe much to Paul's mouth; Paul's mouth owed its power to prayer.

How manifold, illimitable, valuable, and helpful prayer is to the preacher in so many ways, at so many points, in every way! One great value is, it helps his heart.

Praying makes the preacher a heart preacher. Prayer puts the preacher's heart into the preacher's sermon; prayer puts the preacher's sermon into the preacher's heart.

The heart makes the preacher. Men of great hearts are great preachers. Men of bad hearts may do a measure of good, but this is rare. The hireling and the stranger may help the sheep at some points, but it is the good shepherd with the good shepherd's heart who will bless the sheep and answer the full measure of the shepherd's place.

We have emphasized sermon-preparation until we have lost sight of the important thing to be prepared—the heart. A prepared heart is much better than a prepared sermon. A prepared heart will make a prepared sermon.

Volumes have been written laying down the mechanics and taste of sermon-making, until we have become possessed with the idea that this scaffolding is the building. The young preacher has been taught to lay out all his strength on the form, taste, and beauty of his sermon as a mechanical and intellectual product. We have thereby cultivated a vicious taste among the people and raised the clamor for talent instead of grace, eloquence instead of piety, rhetoric instead of revelation, reputation and brilliancy instead of holiness. By it we have lost the true idea of preaching, lost preaching power, lost pungent conviction for sin, lost the rich experience and elevated Christian character, lost the authority over consciences and lives which always results from genuine preaching.

It would not do to say that preachers study too much. Some of them do not study at all; others do not study enough. Numbers do not study the right way to show themselves workmen approved of God. But our great lack is not in head culture, but in heart culture; not lack of knowledge but lack of holiness is our sad and telling defect—not that we know too much, but that we do not meditate on God and His Word and watch and fast and pray enough. The heart is the great hindrance to our preaching. Words pregnant with divine truth find in our hearts nonconductors; arrested, they fall shorn and powerless.

Can ambition, which lusts after praise and place, preach the gospel of Him who made Himself of no reputation and took on Him the form of a servant? Can the proud, the vain, the egotistical preach the gospel of Him who was meek and lowly? Can the bad-tempered, passionate, selfish, hard, worldly man preach the system that teems with long-suffering, self-denial, tenderness, which imperatively demands separation from enmity and crucifixion to the world? Can the hireling official, heartless, perfunctory, preach the gospel that demands the shepherd to give his life for the sheep? Can the covetous man, who counts salary and money, preach the gospel till he has gleaned his heart and can say in the spirit of Christ and Paul in the words of Wesley: "I count it dung and dross; I trample it under my feet; I (yet not I, but the grace of God in me) esteem it just as the mire of the streets, I desire it not, I seek it not?" God's revelation does not need the light of human genius, the polish and strength of human culture, the brilliancy of human thought, the force of human brains to adorn or enforce it; but it does demand the simplicity, the docility, humility, and faith of a child's heart.

It was this surrender and subordination of intellect and genius to the divine and spiritual forces that made Paul peerless among the apostles. It was this that gave Wesley his power and radicated his labors in the history of humanity. This gave to Loyola the strength to arrest the retreating forces of Catholicism.

Our great need is heart-preparation. Luther held it as an axiom: "He who has prayed well has studied well." We do not say that men are not to think and use their intellects; but *he will use his intellect best who cultivates his heart most*. We do not say that preachers should not be students; but we do say that their great study should be the Bible, and he studies the Bible best who has kept his heart with diligence. We do not say that the preacher should not know men, but he will be the greater adept in human nature who has fathomed the depths and intricacies of his own heart. We do say that while the channel of preaching is the mind, its fountain is the heart; you may broaden and deepen the channel, but if you do not look well to the purity and depth of the fountain, you will have a dry or polluted channel. We do say that almost any man of common intelligence has sense enough to preach the gospel, but very few have grace enough to do so. We do say that he who has struggled with his own heart and conquered it; who has taught it humility, faith, love, truth, mercy, sympathy, courage; who can pour the rich treasures of the heart thus trained, through a manly intellect, all surcharged with the power of the gospel on the consciences of his hearers—such a one will be the truest, most successful preacher in the esteem of his Lord.

CHAPTER 13

Grace From the Heart Rather Than the Head

The heart is the Savior of the world. Heads do not save. Genius, brains, brilliancy, strength, natural gifts do not save. The gospel flows through hearts. All the mightiest forces are heart forces. All the sweetest and loveliest graces are heart graces. Great hearts make great characters; great hearts make divine characters. God is love. There is nothing greater than love, nothing greater than God. Hearts make Heaven; Heaven is love. There is nothing higher, nothing sweeter, than Heaven. It is the heart and not the head that makes God's great preachers. The heart counts much every way in religion. The heart must speak from the pulpit. The heart must hear in the pew. In fact, we serve God with our hearts. Head homage does not pass current in Heaven.

We believe that one of the serious and most popular errors of the modern pulpit is the putting of more thought than prayer, of more head than of heart in its sermons. Big hearts make big preachers; good hearts make good preachers. A theological school to enlarge and cultivate the heart is the golden desideratum of the gospel. The pastor binds his people to him and rules his people by his heart. They may admire his gifts, they may be proud of his ability, they may be affected for the time by his sermons; but the stronghold of his power is his heart. His scepter is love. The throne of his power is his heart.

The good shepherd gives his life for the sheep. Heads never make martyrs. It is the heart that surrenders the life to love and fidelity. It takes great courage to be a faithful pastor, but the heart alone can supply this courage. Gifts and genius may be brave, but it is the gifts and genius of the heart and not of the head.

It is easier to fill the head than it is to prepare the heart. It is easier to make a brain sermon than a heart sermon. It was heart that drew the Son of God from Heaven. It is heart that will draw men to Heaven. Men of heart is what the world needs to sympathize with its woe, to kiss away its sorrows, to compassionate its misery, and to alleviate its pain. Christ was eminently the man of sorrows, because He was preeminently the man of heart.

"Give me thy heart," is God's requisition of men. "Give me thy heart!" is man's demand of man.

A professional ministry is a heartless ministry. When salary plays a great part in the ministry, the heart plays little part. We may make preaching our business, and not put our hearts in the business. He who puts self to the front in his preaching puts heart to the rear. He who does not sow with his heart in his study will never reap a harvest for God. The closet is the heart's study. We will learn more about how to preach and what to preach there than we can learn in our libraries. "Jesus wept" is the shortest and biggest verse in the Bible. It is he who goes forth weeping (not preaching great sermons), bearing precious seed, who shall come again rejoicing, bringing his sheaves with him.

Praying gives sense, brings wisdom, broadens and strengthens the mind. The closet is a perfect schoolteacher and schoolhouse for the preacher. Thought is not only brightened and clarified in prayer, but thought is born in prayer. We can learn more in an hour praying, when praying indeed, than from many hours in the study. Books are in the closet that can be found and read nowhere else. Revelations are made in the closet that are made nowhere else.

CHAPTER 14

Unction, a Necessity

Alexander Knox, a Christian philosopher of the days of Wesley, not an adherent but a strong personal friend of Wesley, and with much spiritual sympathy with the Wesleyan movement, writes:

> It is strange and lamentable, but I verily believe the fact to be that except among Methodists and Methodistical clergyman, there is not much interesting preaching in England. The clergy, too generally have absolutely lost the art. There is, I conceive, in the great laws of the moral world a kind of secret understanding like the affinities in chemistry, between rightly promulgated religious truth and the deepest feelings of the human mind. Where the one is duly exhibited, the other will respond. Did not our hearts burn within us?—but to this devout feeling is indispensable in the speaker. Now, I am obliged to state from my own observation that this *onction*, as the French not unfitly term it, is beyond all comparison more likely to be found in England in a Methodist conventicle than in a parish Church. This, and this alone, seems really to be that which fills the Methodist houses and thins the

Churches. I am, I verily think, no enthusiast; I am a most sincere and cordial churchman, a humble disciple of the School of Hale and Boyle, of Burnet and Leighton. Now I must aver that when I was in this country, two years ago, I did not hear a single preacher who taught me like my own great masters but such as are deemed Methodistical. And I now despair of getting an atom of heart instruction from any other quarter. The Methodist preachers (however I may not always approve of all their expressions) do most assuredly diffuse this true religion and undefiled. I felt real pleasure last Sunday. I can bear witness that the preacher did at once speak the words of truth and soberness. There was no eloquence—the honest man never dreamed of such a thing—but there was far better: a cordial communication of vitalized truth. I say vitalized because what he declared to others it was impossible not to feel he lived on himself.

This unction is the art of preaching. The preacher who never had this unction never had the art of preaching. The preacher who has lost this unction has lost the art of preaching. Whatever other arts he may have and retain—the art of sermon-making, the art of eloquence, the art of great, clear thinking, the art of pleasing an audience—he has lost the divine art of preaching. This unction makes God's truth powerful and interesting, draws and attracts, edifies, convicts, saves.

This unction vitalizes God's revealed truth, makes it living and life-giving. Even God's truth spoken without this unction is light, dead, and deadening. Though abounding in truth, though weighty with thought, though sparkling with rhetoric, though pointed by logic, though powerful by earnestness, without this divine unction it issues in death and not in life. Mr. Spurgeon says:

> I wonder how long we might beat our brains before we could plainly put into word what is meant by preaching with unction. Yet he who preaches knows its presence, and he who hears soon detects its absence. Samaria, in famine, typifies a discourse without it.

Jerusalem, with her feast of fat things, full of marrow, may represent a sermon enriched with it. Every one knows what the freshness of the morning is when orient pearls abound on every blade of grass, but who can describe it, much less produce it of itself? Such is the mystery of spiritual anointing. We know, but we cannot tell to others what it is. It is as easy as it is foolish, to counterfeit it. Unction is a thing that you cannot manufacture, and its counterfeits are worse than worthless. Yet it is, in itself, priceless, and beyond measure needful if you would edify believers and bring sinners to Christ.

CHAPTER 15

Unction, the Mark of True Gospel Preaching

Unction is that indefinable, indescribable something that an old, renowned Scotch preacher describes thus:

> There is sometimes somewhat in preaching that cannot be ascribed either to matter or expression, and cannot be described what it is, or from whence it cometh, but with a sweet violence it pierceth into the heart and affections and comes immediately from the Word; but if there be any way to obtain such a thing, it is by the heavenly disposition of the speaker.

We call it unction. It is this unction that makes the word of God "quick and powerful, and sharper than any two-edged sword, piercing even to the dividing asunder of soul and spirit, and of the joints and marrow, and a discerner of the thoughts and intents of the heart." It is this unction that gives the words of the preacher such point, sharpness, and power, and which creates such friction and stir in many a dead congregation. The same truths have been told in the strictness of the letter, smooth as human oil could make them; but no signs of life, not a pulse throb; all as peaceful as the grave and as dead. The same preacher in the meanwhile receives a baptism of this unction, the divine inflatus is on him, the letter of the Word has been embellished and fired by this mysterious power, and the throbbings of life begin— life that receives or life that resists. The unction pervades and convicts the conscience and breaks the heart.

This divine unction is the feature that separates and distinguishes true gospel preaching from all other methods of presenting the truth, and that creates a wide spiritual chasm between the preacher who has it and the one who has it not. It backs and impregns revealed truth with all the energy of God. Unction is simply putting God in His own word and on His own preachers. By mighty and great prayerfulness and by continual prayerfulness, it is all potential and personal to the preacher; it inspires and clarifies his intellect, gives insight and grasp and projecting power; it gives to the preacher heart power, which is greater than head power; and tenderness, purity, force flow from the heart by it. Enlargement, freedom, fullness of thought, directness and simplicity of utterance are the fruits of this unction.

Often earnestness is mistaken for this unction. He who has the divine unction will be earnest in the very spiritual nature of things, but there may be a vast deal of earnestness without the least mixture of unction.

Earnestness and unction look alike from some points of view. Earnestness may be readily and without detection substituted or mistaken for unction. It requires a spiritual eye and a spiritual taste to discriminate.

Earnestness may be sincere, serious, ardent, and persevering. It goes at a thing with good will, pursues it with perseverance, and urges it with ardor; puts force in it. But all these forces do not rise higher than the mere human. The *man* is in it—the whole man, with all that he has of will and heart, of brain and genius, of planning and working and talking. He has set himself to some purpose that has mastered him, and he pursues to master it. There may be none of God in it. There may be little of God in it, because there is so much of the man in it. He may present pleas in advocacy of his earnest purpose that please or touch and move or overwhelm with conviction of their importance; and in all this earnestness may move along earthly ways, being propelled by human forces only, its altar made by earthly hands and its fire kindled by earthly flames. It is said of a rather famous preacher of gifts, whose construction of Scripture was to his fancy or purpose, that he "grew very eloquent over his own exegesis." So men grow exceeding earnest over their own plans or movements. Earnestness may be selfishness simulated.

What of unction? It is the indefinable in preaching that makes it preaching. It is that which distinguishes and separates preaching from all mere human addresses. It is the divine in preaching. It makes the preaching sharp to those who need sharpness. It distills as the dew to those who need to be refreshed. It is well described as:

A two-edged sword
Of heavenly temper keen,

And double were the wounds it made
Wherever it glanced between.

'Twas death to silt; 'twas life
To all who mourned for sin.

It kindled and it silenced strife,
Made war and peace within.

This unction comes to the preacher not in the study but in the closet. It is Heaven's distillation in answer to prayer. It is the sweetest exhalation of the Holy Spirit. It impregnates, suffuses, softens, percolates, cuts, and soothes. It carries the Word like dynamite, like salt, like sugar; makes the Word a soother, an arranger, a revealer, a searcher; makes the hearer a culprit or a saint, makes him weep like a child and live like a giant; opens his heart and his purse as gently, yet as strongly as the spring opens the leaves. This unction is not the gift of genius. It is not found in the halls of learning. No eloquence can woo it. No industry can win it. No prelatical hands can confer it. It is the gift of God—the signet set to His own messengers. It is Heaven's knighthood given to the chosen true and brave ones who have sought this anointed honor through many an hour of tearful, wrestling prayer.

Earnestness is good and impressive; genius is gifted and great. Thought kindles and inspires, but it takes a diviner endowment, a more powerful energy than earnestness or genius or thought to break the chains of sin, to win estranged and depraved hearts to God, to repair the breaches and restore the Church to her old ways of purity and power. Nothing but this holy unction can do this.

CHAPTER 16

Much Prayer, the Price of Unction

In the Christian system, unction is the anointing of the Holy Ghost, separating unto God's work and qualifying for it. This unction is the one divine enablement by which the preacher accomplishes the peculiar and saving ends of preaching. Without this unction there are no true spiritual results accomplished; the results and forces in preaching do not rise above the results of unsanctified speech. Without unction the former is as potent as the pulpit.

This divine unction on the preacher generates through the Word of God the spiritual results that flow from the gospel; and without this unction, these results are not secured. Many pleasant impressions may be made, but these all fall far below the ends of gospel preaching. This unction may be simulated. There are many things that look like it, there are many results that resemble its effects; but they are foreign to its results and to its nature. The fervor or softness excited by a pathetic or emotional sermon may look like the movements of the divine unction, but they have no pungent, perpetrating heart-breaking force. No heart-healing balm is there in these surface, sympathetic, emotional movements; they are not radical, neither sin-searching nor sin-curing.

This divine unction is the one distinguishing feature that separates true gospel preaching from all other methods of presenting truth. It backs and interpenetrates the revealed truth with all the force of God. It illumines the Word and broadens and enrichens the intellect and empowers it to grasp and apprehend the Word. It qualifies the preacher's heart, and brings it to that condition of tenderness, of purity, of force and light that are necessary to secure the highest results. This unction gives to the preacher liberty and enlargement of thought and soul—a freedom, fullness, and directness of utterance that can be secured by no other process.

Without this unction on the preacher the gospel has no more power to propagate itself than any other system of truth. This is the seal of its divinity. Unction in the preacher puts God in the gospel. Without the unction, God is absent, and the gospel is left to the low and unsatisfactory forces that the ingenuity, interest, or talents of men can devise to enforce and project its doctrines.

It is in this element that the pulpit oftener fails than in any other element. Just at this all-important point it lapses. Learning it may have, brilliancy and eloquence may delight and charm, sensation or less offensive methods may bring the populace in crowds, mental power may impress and enforce truth with all its resources; but without this unction, each and all these will be but as the fretful assault of the waters on a Gibraltar. Spray and foam may cover and spangle; but the rocks are there still, unimpressed and unimpressible. The human heart can no more be swept of its hardness and sin by these human forces than these rocks can be swept away by the ocean's ceaseless flow.

This unction is the consecration force, and its presence the continuous test of that consecration. It is this divine anointing on the preacher that secures his consecration to God and His work. Other forces and motives may call him to the work, but this only is consecration. A separation to God's work by the power of the Holy Spirit is the only consecration recognized by God as legitimate.

The unction, the divine unction, this heavenly anointing, is what the pulpit needs and must have. This divine and heavenly oil put on it by the imposition of God's hand must soften and lubricate the whole man—heart, head, spirit—until it separates him with a mighty separation from all earthly, secular, worldly, selfish motives and aims, separating him to everything that is pure and Godlike.

It is the presence of this unction on the preacher that creates the stir and friction in many a congregation. The same truths have been told in the strictness of the letter, but no ruffle has been seen, no pain or pulsation felt. All is quiet as a graveyard. Another preacher comes, and this mysterious influence is on him; the letter of the Word has been fired by the Spirit; the throes of a mighty movement are felt; it is the unction that pervades and stirs the conscience and breaks the heart. Unctionless preaching makes everything hard, dry, acrid, dead.

This unction is not a memory or an era of the past only; it is a present, realized, conscious fact. It belongs to the experience of the man as well as to his preaching. It is that which transforms him into the image of his divine Master, as well as that by which he declares the truths of Christ with power. It is so much the power in the ministry as to make all else seem feeble and vain without it, and by its presence to atone for the absence of all other and feebler forces.

This unction is not an inalienable gift. It is a conditional gift, and its presence is perpetuated and increased by the same process by which it was at first secured; by unceasing prayer to God, by impassioned desires after God, by estimating it, by seeking it with tireless ardor, by deeming all else loss and failure without it.

How and whence comes this unction? Direct from God in answer to prayer. Praying hearts only are the hearts filled with this holy oil; praying lips only are anointed with this divine unction.

Prayer, much prayer, is the price of preaching unction; prayer, much prayer, is the one, sole condition of keeping this unction. Without unceasing prayer the unction never comes to the preacher. Without perseverance in prayer, the unction, like the manna overkept, breeds worms.

CHAPTER 17

Prayer Marks Spiritual Leadership

The apostles knew the necessity and worth of prayer to their ministry. They knew that their high commission as apostles, instead of relieving them from the necessity of prayer, committed them to it by a more urgent need; so that they were exceedingly jealous else some other important work should exhaust their time and prevent their praying as they ought; so they appointed laymen to look after the delicate and engrossing duties of ministering to the poor, that they (the apostles) might, unhindered, "give themselves continually to prayer and to the ministry of the word." Prayer is put first, and their relation to prayer is put most strongly—"give themselves to it," making a business of it, surrendering themselves to praying, putting fervor, urgency, perseverance, and time in it.

How holy, apostolic men devoted themselves to this divine work of prayer! "Night and day praying exceedingly," says Paul. "We will give ourselves continually to prayer" is the consensus of apostolic devotement. How these New Testament preachers laid themselves out in prayer for God's people! How they put God in full force into their Churches by their praying! These holy apostles did not vainly fancy that they had met their high and solemn duties by delivering faithfully God's word, but their preaching was made to stick and tell by the ardor and insistence of their praying. Apostolic praying was as taxing, toilsome, and imperative as apostolic preaching. They prayed mightily day and night to bring their people to the highest regions of faith and holiness. They prayed mightier still to hold them to this high spiritual altitude. The preacher who has never learned in the school of Christ the high and divine art of intercession for his people will never learn the art of preaching, though homiletics be poured into him by the ton, and though he be the most gifted genius in sermon-making and sermon-delivery.

The prayers of apostolic, saintly leaders do much in making saints of those who are not apostles. If the Church leaders in after years had been as particular and fervent in praying for their people as the apostles were, the sad, dark times of worldliness and apostasy may not have marred the history and eclipsed the glory and arrested the advance of the Church. Apostolic praying makes apostolic saints and keeps apostolic times of purity and power in the Church.

What loftiness of soul, what purity and elevation of motive, what unselfishness, what self-sacrifice, what exhaustive toil, what ardor of spirit, what divine tact are requisite to be an intercessor for men!

The preacher is to lay himself out in prayer for his people; not that they might be saved, simply, but that they be mightily saved. The apostles laid themselves out in prayer that their saints might be perfect; not that they should have a little relish for the things of God, but that they "might be filled with all the fullness of God." Paul did not rely on his apostolic preaching to secure this end, but "for this cause he bowed his knees to the Father of our Lord Jesus Christ." Paul's praying carried Paul's converts farther along the highway of sainthood than Paul's preaching did. Epaphras did as much or more by prayer for the Colossian saints than by his preaching. He labored fervently always in prayer for them that "they might stand perfect and complete in all the will of God."

Preachers are preeminently God's leaders. They are primarily responsible for the condition of the Church. They shape its character, give tone and direction to its life.

Much in every way depends on these leaders. They shape the times and the institutions. The Church is divine, the treasure it encases is heavenly, but it bears the imprint of the human. The treasure is in earthen vessels, and it smacks of the vessel. The Church of God makes, or is made by, its leaders. Whether it makes them or is made by them, it will be what its leaders are; spiritual if they are so, secular if they are, conglomerate if its leaders are. Israel's kings gave character to Israel's piety. A church rarely revolts against or rises above the religion of its leaders. Strongly spiritual leaders; men of holy might, at the lead, are tokens of God's favor; disaster and weakness follow the wake of feeble or worldly leaders. Israel had fallen low when God gave children to be their princes and babes to rule over them. No happy state is predicted by the prophets when children oppress God's Israel and women rule over them. Times of spiritual leadership are times of great spiritual prosperity to the Church.

Prayer is one of the eminent characteristics of strong spiritual leadership. Men of mighty prayer are men of might and mold things. Their power with God has the conquering tread.

How can a man preach who does not get his message fresh from God in the closet? How can he preach without having his faith quickened, his vision cleared, and his heart warmed by his closeting with God? Alas, for the pulpit lips that are untouched by this closet flame. Dry and unctionless they will ever be, and truths divine will never come with power from such lips. As far as the real interests of religion are concerned, a pulpit without a closet will always be a barren thing.

A preacher may preach in an official, entertaining, or learned way without prayer, but between this kind of preaching and sowing God's precious seed with holy hands and prayerful, weeping hearts there is an immeasurable distance.

A prayerless ministry is the undertaker for all God's truth and for God's Church. He may have the most costly casket and the most beautiful flowers, but it is a funeral, notwithstanding the charmful array. A prayerless Christian will never learn God's truth; a prayerless ministry will never be able to teach God's truth. Ages of millennial glory have been lost by a prayerless Church. The coming of our Lord has been postponed indefinitely by a prayerless Church. Hell has enlarged herself and filled her dire caves in the presence of the dead service of a prayerless Church.

The best, the greatest offering is an offering of prayer. If the preachers of the twentieth century will learn well the lesson of prayer, and use fully the power of prayer, the millennium will come to its noon ere the century closes. "Pray without ceasing" is the trumpet call to the preachers of the twentieth century. If the twentieth century will get their texts, their thoughts, their words, their sermons in their closets, the next century will find a new Heaven and a new earth. The old sin-stained and sin-eclipsed heaven and earth will pass away under the power of a praying ministry.

CHAPTER 18

Preachers Need the Prayers of the People

Somehow the practice of praying in particular for the preacher has fallen into disuse or become discounted. Occasionally have we heard the practice arraigned as a disparagement of the ministry, being a public declaration by those who do it of the inefficiency of the ministry. It offends the pride of learning and self-sufficiency, perhaps, and these ought to be offended and rebuked in a ministry that is so derelict as to allow them to exist.

Prayer, to the preacher, is not simply the duty of his profession, a privilege, but it is a necessity. Air is not more necessary to the lungs than prayer is to the preacher. It is absolutely necessary for the preacher to pray. It is an absolute necessity that the preacher be prayed for. These two propositions are wedded into a union that ought never to know any divorce: *the preacher must pray; the preacher must be prayed for.* It will take all the praying he can do, and all the praying he can get done, to meet the fearful responsibilities and gain the largest, truest success in his great work. The true preacher, next to the cultivation of the spirit and fact of prayer in himself, in their intensest form, covets with a great covetousness the prayers of God's people.

The holier a man is, the more does he estimate prayer; the clearer does he see that God gives Himself to the praying ones, and that the measure of God's revelation to the soul is the measure of the soul's longing, importunate prayer for God. Salvation never finds its way to a prayerless heart. The Holy Spirit never abides in a prayerless spirit. Preaching never edifies a prayerless soul. Christ knows nothing of prayerless Christians. The gospel cannot be projected by a prayerless preacher. Gifts, talents, education, eloquence, God's call, cannot abate the demand of prayer, but only intensify the necessity for the preacher to pray and to be prayed for. The more the preacher's eyes are opened to the nature, responsibility, and difficulties in his work, the more will he see, and if he be a true preacher the more will he feel, the necessity of prayer; not only the increasing demand to pray himself, but to call on others to help him by their prayers.

Paul is an illustration of this. If any man could project the gospel by dint of personal force, by brain power, by culture, by personal grace, by God's apostolic commission, God's extraordinary call, that man was Paul. That the preacher must be a man given to prayer, Paul is an eminent example. That the true apostolic preacher must have the prayers of other good people to give to his ministry its full quota of success, Paul is a preeminent example. He asks, he covets, he pleads in an impassioned way for the help of all God's saints. He knew that in the spiritual realm, as elsewhere, in union there is strength; that the concentration and aggregation of faith, desire, and prayer increased the volume of spiritual force until it became overwhelming and irresistible in its power.

Units of prayer combined, like drops of water, make an ocean that defies resistance. So Paul, with his clear and full apprehension of spiritual dynamics, determined to make his ministry as impressive, as eternal, as irresistible as the ocean, by gathering all the scattered units of prayer and precipitating them on his ministry. May not the solution of Paul's preeminence in labors and results, and impress on the Church and the world, be found in this fact that he was able to center on himself and his ministry more of prayer than others? To his brethren at Rome he wrote: *"Now I beseech you, brethren, for the Lord Jesus Christ's sake, and for the love of the Spirit, that ye strive together with me in prayers to God for me." To the Ephesians he says: "Praying always with all prayer and supplication in the Spirit, and watching thereunto with all perseverance and supplication for all saints; and for me, that utterance may be given unto me, that I may open my mouth boldly, to make known the mystery of the gospel."* To the Colossians he emphasizes: *"Withal praying also for us, that God would open unto us a door of utterance, to speak the mystery of Christ, for which I am also in bonds: that I may make it manifest as I ought to speak."* To the Thessalonians he says sharply, strongly: *"Brethren, pray for us."* Paul calls on the Corinthian Church to help him: *"Ye also helping together by prayer for us."*

This was to be part of their work. They were to be the helping hand of prayer. Paul, in an additional and closing charge to the Thessalonian Church about the importance and necessity of their prayers, says: *"Finally, brethren, pray for us, that the word of the Lord may have free course, and be glorified, even as it is with you: and that we may be delivered from unreasonable and wicked men."* He impresses the Philippians that all his trials and opposition can be made subservient to the spread of the gospel by the efficiency of their prayers for him. Philemon was to prepare a lodging for him, for through Philemon's prayer Paul was to be his guest.

Paul's attitude on this question illustrates his humility and his deep insight into the spiritual forces that project the gospel. More than this, it teaches a lesson for all times, that if Paul was so dependent on the prayers of God's saints to give his ministry success, how much greater the necessity that the prayers of God's saints be centered on the ministry of today!

Paul did not feel that this urgent plea for prayer was to lower his dignity, lessen his influence, or depreciate his piety. What if it did? Let dignity go, let influence be destroyed, let his reputation be marred—he must have their prayers. Called, commissioned, chief of the Apostles as he was, all his equipment was imperfect without the prayers of his people. He wrote letters everywhere, urging them to pray for him. Do you pray for your preacher? Do you pray for him in secret? **Public prayers are of little worth unless they are founded on or followed up by private praying.** The praying ones are to the preacher as Aaron and Hur were to Moses. They hold up his hands and decide the issue that is so fiercely raging around them.

The plea and purpose of the apostles were to put the Church to praying. They did not ignore the grace of cheerful giving. They were not ignorant of the place that religious activity and work occupied in the spiritual life; but not one nor all of these, in apostolic estimate or urgency, could at all compare in necessity and importance with prayer. The most sacred and urgent pleas were used, the most fervid exhortations, the most comprehensive and arousing words were uttered to enforce the all-important obligation and necessity of prayer.

"Put the saints everywhere to praying" is the burden of the apostolic effort and the keynote of apostolic success. Jesus Christ had striven to do this in the days of His personal ministry. As He was moved by infinite compassion at the ripened fields of earth perishing for lack of laborers and pausing in His own praying—He tries to awaken the stupid sensibilities of His disciples to the duty of prayer as He charges them, *"Pray ye the Lord of the harvest that He will send forth laborers into His harvest." "And He spake a parable unto them to this end, that men ought always to pray and not to faint."*

CHAPTER 19

Deliberation Necessary to Largest Results From Prayer

Our devotions are not measured by the clock, but time is of their essence. The ability to wait and stay and press belongs essentially to our intercourse with God. Hurry, everywhere unseeming and damaging, is so to an alarming extent in the great business of communion with God. Short devotions are the bane of deep piety. Calmness, grasp, strength, are never the companions of hurry. Short devotions deplete spiritual vigor, arrest spiritual progress, sap spiritual foundations, blight the root and bloom of spiritual life. They are the prolific source of backsliding, the sure indication of a superficial piety; they deceive, blight, rot the seed, and impoverish the soil.

It is true that Bible prayers in word and print are short, but the praying men of the Bible were with God through many a sweet and holy wrestling hour. They won by few words but long waiting. The prayers Moses records may be short, but Moses prayed to God with fastings and mighty cryings 40 days and nights.

The statement of Elijah's praying may be condensed to a few brief paragraphs, but doubtless Elijah, who when "praying he prayed," spent many hours of fiery struggle and lofty intercourse with God before he could, with assured boldness, say to Ahab, "There shall not be dew nor rain these years, but according to my word." The verbal brief of Paul's prayers is short, but Paul "prayed night and day exceedingly." The "Lord's Prayer" is a divine epitome for infant lips, but the man Christ Jesus prayed many an all-night ere His work was done; and His all-night and long-sustained devotions gave to His work its finish and perfection, and to His character the fullness and glory of its divinity.

Spiritual work is taxing work, and men are loath to do it. Praying, true praying, costs an outlay of serious attention and of time, which flesh and blood do not relish. Few persons are made of such strong fiber that they will make a costly outlay when surface work will pass as well in the market. We can habituate ourselves to our beggarly praying until it looks well to us, at least it keeps up a decent form and quiets conscience—the deadliest of opiates! We can slight our praying, and not realize the peril till the foundations are gone. Hurried devotions make weak faith, feeble convictions, questionable piety. *To be little with God is to be little for God.* To cut short the praying makes the whole religious character short, scrimp, niggardly, and slovenly.

It takes good time for the full flow of God into the spirit. Short devotions cut the pipe of God's full flow. It takes time in the secret places to get the full revelation of God. Little time and hurry mar the picture.

Henry Martyn laments that "want of private devotional reading and shortness of prayer through incessant sermon-making had produced much strangeness between God and his soul." He judged that he had dedicated too much time to public ministrations and too little to private communion with God. He was much impressed to set apart times for fasting and to devote times for solemn prayer. Resulting from this he records: "Was assisted this morning to pray for two hours." Said William Wilberforce, the peer of kings: "I must secure more time for private devotions. I have been living far too public for me. The shortening of private devotions starves the soul; it grows lean and faint. I have been keeping too late hours." Of a failure in Parliament he says: "Let me record my grief and shame, and all, probably, from private devotions having been contracted, and so God let me stumble." More solitude and earlier hours was his remedy.

More time and early hours for prayer would act like magic to revive and invigorate many a decayed spiritual life. More time and early hours for prayer would be manifest in holy living. A holy life would not be so rare or so difficult a thing if our devotions were not so short and hurried. A Christly temper in its sweet and passionless fragrance would not be so alien and hopeless a heritage if our closet stay were lengthened and intensified. We live shabbily because we pray meanly. Plenty of time to feast in our closets will bring marrow and fatness to our lives. Our ability to stay with God in our closet measures our ability to stay with God out of the closet.

Hasty closet visits are deceptive, defaulting. We are not only deluded by them, but we are losers by them in many ways and in many rich legacies. Tarrying in the closet instructs and wins. We are taught by it, and the greatest victories are often the results of great waiting—waiting till words and plans are exhausted, and silent and patient waiting gains the crown. Jesus Christ asks with an affronted emphasis, "Shall not God avenge His own elect which cry day and night unto Him?"

To pray is the greatest thing we can do; and to do it well there must be calmness, time, and deliberation; otherwise it is degraded into the littlest and meanest of things. True praying has the largest results for good; and poor praying, the least. We cannot do too much of real praying; we cannot do too little of the sham. We must learn anew the worth of prayer, enter anew the school of prayer. There is nothing that it takes more time to learn. And if we would learn the wondrous art, we must not give a fragment here and there—"A little talk with Jesus," as the tiny saintlets sing—but we must demand and hold with iron grasp the best hours of the day for God and prayer, or there will be no praying worth the name.

This, however, is not a day of prayer. Few men there are who pray. Prayer is defamed by preacher and priest. In these days of hurry and bustle, of electricity and steam, men will not take time to pray. Preachers there are who "say prayers" as a part of their program, on regular or state occasions; but who "stirs himself up to take hold upon God"? Who prays as Jacob prayed—till he is crowned as a prevailing, princely intercessor? Who prays as Elijah prayed—till all the locked-up forces of nature were unsealed and a famine-stricken land bloomed as the garden of God? Who prayed as Jesus Christ prayed as out upon the mountain He "continued all night in prayer to God"?

The apostles "gave themselves to prayer"—the most difficult thing to get men or even the preachers to do. Laymen there are who will give their money—some of them in rich abundance—but they will not "give themselves" to prayer, without which their money is but a curse. There are plenty of preachers who will preach and deliver great and eloquent addresses on the need of revival and the spread of the Kingdom of God, but not many there are who will do that without which all preaching and organizing are worse than vain—pray. It is out of date, almost a lost art, and the greatest benefactor this age could have is the man who will bring the preachers and the Church back to prayer.

CHAPTER 20

A Praying Pulpit Begets a Praying Pew

Only glimpses of the great importance of prayer could the apostles get before Pentecost. But the Spirit coming and filling on Pentecost elevated prayer to its vital and all-commanding position in the gospel of Christ. The call now of prayer to every saint is the Spirit's loudest and most exigent call. Sainthood's piety is made, refined, perfected, by prayer. The gospel moves with slow and timid pace when the saints are not at their prayers early and late and long.

Where are the Christly leaders who can teach the modern saints how to pray and put them at it? Do we know we are raising up a prayerless set of saints? Where are the apostolic leaders who can put God's people to praying? Let them come to the front and do the work, and it will be the greatest work that can be done. An increase of educational facilities and a great increase of money force will be the direst curse to religion if they are not sanctified by more and better praying than we are doing.

More praying will not come as a matter of course. The campaign for the twentieth or thirtieth century fund will not help our praying but hinder if we are not careful. Nothing but a specific effort from a praying leadership will avail. The chief ones must lead in the apostolic effort to radicate the vital importance and *fact* of prayer in the heart and life of the Church. None but praying leaders can have praying followers. Praying apostles will beget praying saints. A praying pulpit will beget praying pews.

We do greatly need somebody who can set the saints to this business of praying. We are not a generation of praying saints. Non-praying saints are a beggarly gang of saints who have neither the ardor nor the beauty nor the power of saints. Who will restore this breach? The greatest will he be of reformers and apostles, who can set the Church to praying.

We put it as our most sober judgment that the great need of the Church in this and all ages is men of such commanding faith, of such unsullied holiness, of such marked spiritual vigor and consuming zeal, that their prayers, faith, lives, and ministry will be of such a radical and aggressive form as to work spiritual revolutions that will form eras in individual and Church life.

We do not mean men who get up sensational stirs by novel devices, nor those who attract by a pleasing entertainment; but men who can stir things, and work revolutions by the preaching of God's Word and by the power of the Holy Ghost, revolutions that change the whole current of things.

Natural ability and educational advantages do not figure as factors in this matter; but capacity for faith, the ability to pray, the power of thorough consecration, the ability of self-littleness, an absolute losing of one's self in God's glory, and an ever-present and insatiable yearning and seeking after all the fullness of God—men who can set the Church ablaze for God; not in a noisy, showy way, but with an intense and quiet heat that melts and moves everything for God.

God can work wonders if He can get a suitable man. Men can work wonders if they can get God to lead them. The full endowment of the spirit that turned the world upside down would be eminently useful in these latter days. Men who can stir things mightily for God, whose spiritual revolutions change the whole aspect of things, are the universal need of the Church.

The Church has never been without these men; they adorn its history; they are the standing miracles of the divinity of the Church; their example and history are an unfailing inspiration and blessing. An increase in their number and power should be our prayer.

That which has been done in spiritual matters can be done again, and be better done. This was Christ's view. He said, *"Verily, verily, I say unto you, he that believeth on Me, the works that I do shall he do also; and greater works than these shall he do; because I go unto My Father."* **The past has not exhausted the possibilities nor the demands for doing great things for God.** The Church that is dependent on its past history for its miracles of power and grace is a fallen Church.

God wants elect men—men out of whom self and the world have gone by a severe crucifixion, by a bankruptcy that has so totally ruined self and the world that there is neither hope nor desire of recovery; men who by this insolvency and crucifixion have turned toward God perfect hearts.

Let us pray ardently that God's promise to prayer may be more than realized.

About the Author

James (Jim) W. Goll is the cofounder of Encounters Network (formerly Ministry to the Nations) with his wife Michal Ann. They are members of the Harvest International Ministries Apostolic Team and contributing writers for *Kiros Magazine* and other periodicals. James and Michal Ann have four wonderful children and live in the beautiful rolling hills of Franklin, Tennessee.

James has produced several study guides on subjects such as Equipping in the Prophetic, Blueprints for Prayer, and Empowered for Ministry, which are all available through the Encounters Resource Center.

Other books by James and Michal Ann Goll include:

- ❖ Fire on the Altar
- ❖ Kneeling on the Promises
- ❖ The Lost Art of Practicing His Presence
- ❖ Exodus Cry
- ❖ Elijah's Revolution

- ❖ The Coming Prophetic Revolution
- ❖ A Call to Courage
- ❖ A Call to the Secret Place
- ❖ Compassion
- ❖ Intercession
- ❖ The Beginner's Guide to Hearing God
- ❖ The Seer
- ❖ God Encounters
- ❖ Praying for Israel's Destiny

For more information, contact:

ENCOUNTERS NETWORK
P.O. Box 1653
Franklin, TN 37057
Office Phone: 615-599-5552
Office Fax: 615-599-5554
For orders call: 1-877-200-1604

For more information or to sign up for monthly e-mail communiques, please visit www.encountersnetwork.com or send an e-mail to: info@encountersnetwork.com.

Additional copies of this book and other
book titles from DESTINY IMAGE are
available at your local bookstore.

Call toll-free: 1-800-722-6774.

Send a request for a catalog to:

Destiny Image® Publishers, Inc.
P.O. Box 310
Shippensburg, PA 17257-0310

*"Speaking to the Purposes of God for This
Generation and for the Generations to Come"*

**For a complete list of our titles,
visit us at www.destinyimage.com**